D1325968

THE DAWN
OF WORLD RAILWAYS
1800–1850

Railways of the World in Colour

THE DAWN
OF WORLD RAILWAYS
1800–1850

by
O. S. NOCK

Illustrated by
CLIFFORD and WENDY MEADWAY

LONDON
BLANDFORD PRESS

First published in 1972

© 1972 Blandford Press Ltd
167 High Holborn, London WC1V 6PH

ISBN 0 7137 0563 9

Text printed in Great Britain by
Richard Clay (The Chaucer Press) Ltd, Bungay, Suffolk
Colour section printed by De Ysel Press,
Deventer, Holland

PREFACE

In taking the story of railways back to their very origins the artists and I have had access to a vast amount of contemporary literature, much of it illustrated by very attractive engravings, but naturally lacking entirely in *colour*. And as colour is the very essence of this series of books, the difficulties of research have been greater than ever. It is, in fact, these difficulties that have deferred the appearance of this volume, which chronologically should have been first, to fourth in the order. Fortunately, in the meantime much information has come to light, and as the early volumes have been published readers in many parts of the world have been kind enough to write and provide additional material, and sometimes to enquire why certain areas seem to have escaped our attention. It will now be possible to fill in some of the obvious gaps, notably concerning Japan, in the remaining volumes of the series by exercising a little elasticity in the prescribed dates.

In the present volume I am very grateful to Mr. John H. White, a leading authority on the early history of the steam locomotive in the U.S.A., for his advice and help, though it must be recorded that all authorities do not agree over the vital matter of *colour*. There are disagreements, over items far nearer home, but we hope that, all in all, we have succeeded in giving a representative picture of the early and fascinating period. It is surprising in what unexpected places items of great historical interest are revealed. Just at the time when this particular volume was being compiled some friends in the U S A took me to see that they term a 'grade crossing'—a crossing of two single-line railways on the level, where there was not only a surviving specimen of one of the old 'Highball' signals, but it was still in use, in the year of Grace 1971! Some interesting examples of North American signalling practice, so different from that of Great Britain, are in readiness for the next volume of this series.

Silver Cedars
High Bannerdown,
Batheaston,
BATH

November 1971

INTRODUCTION

If one were to try and trace the beginnings of railways back to basic fundamentals in the form of their major components, the quest could well take us back into the mists of ancient history; for the wheel was one of the earliest mechanical inventions of man. But transport in wheeled vehicles did not begin to earn the title of 'rail-ways' until the beginnings of the Industrial Revolution in Great Britain made it necessary to find means to enable horses to draw a heavier load than hitherto. There is documentary evidence in early engravings, and still more primitive forms of illustration, of wagons running on various crude forms of track in much earlier days than in the latter part of the eighteenth century in England; but for the purpose of this book the Industrial Revolution makes a good springboard. If the small mineral wagons of the day were run on substantially smooth and unyielding tracks it was found that a single horse could often pull two, three or four of them instead of only one, along the rough cart tracks of the day. Some of the earliest rails were made of nothing more durable than hard wood, while other prospectors began to experiment with wrought iron plates. At the same time, methods of guiding had to be devised, for with trains of three or four wagons the path could not be steered as with a horse pulling a single wagon on an ordinary road.

Then the whole situation was changed by James Watt's invention of the steam engine. This was not yet in the form of the locomotive but for stationary use, such as driving machinery. But one very important application of the early Watt engines was for pumping water out of the tin mines in Cornwall. There they came under the scrutiny of that remarkable man,

Richard Trevithick, who, in his dynamic, stop-at-nothing personality, was the very antithesis of the retiring, rather timorous James Watt. He saw that the new power could be made to take the place of horses, and having broken away from Watt's conception using low-pressure steam and condensing the exhaust, and evolved instead the 'puffer' that exhausted steam to atmosphere, he set to work to produce what proved to be the very first locomotive. Despite the difficulty of communications in a country that was still on no more than the threshold of its industrial development, the news of Trevithick's work spread to the north of England, and the gradual evolution of the steam locomotive was continued by such men as George Stephenson, Hedley, Blenkinsop and others. All this early development was entirely for the purpose of carrying coal and minerals. There was no question of carrying passengers by steam-worked railways. Colliery railways, with various forms of primitive rails, were constructed in various parts of Northumberland and Durham to transport coal from the mines to points of shipment on the open coast, or on the estuaries of tidal rivers; but the project that changed the whole trend of events—as much as James Watt's invention —was the incorporation of the Stockton and Darlington Railway as a common carrier. While its prime function was again to carry coal, the company was prepared to carry any kind of freight—and *passengers*.

It was the first public railway in the world; but despite all that had so far been done towards the development of the steam locomotive it was, on its opening in 1825, operated almost entirely by horses.

The company certainly had one locomotive—probably the most powerful and reliable that had been built up to that time —George Stephenson's ever famous *Locomotion*. But all the regular work of the line was done by horses. Passenger 'trains' consisted of but a single coach; but with the well-designed wagons having flanged wheels, and George Stephenson's own type of rails, the horses could pull a good load of coal or other merchandise. The traffic and the geography of the district suited the use of horses. The name of the railway, Stockton and Darlington, was something of a misnomer, because the inland terminus was up in the coal fields near Bishop Auckland, and from there the line descended on something of a gradient. There was no need for any 'haulage' as such on these inclines. The trains included 'dandy carts' in which the horse rode when he was not required for pulling. But although the Stockton and Darlington did not at first advance the art of steam locomotion, its immediate success as a railway fairly 'started something', and within the ensuing fifteen years railways had been opened in the following countries: U.S.A. (1827); France (1828); Germany (1835); Belgium and Canada (1836); Austria (1837); Russia (1838); Holland and Italy (1839).

Despite the success George Stephenson had achieved with the *Locomotion* on the Stockton and Darlington Railway the machine had not reached any degree of sustained reliability, and things were made worse through Stephenson's own personal success. He was already much in demand as a consultant for other railway projects. Promoters in various parts of the country felt that the success of any new railway was assured if George Stephenson could be persuaded to become a shareholder, and he became most deeply involved with the proposed railway between Liverpool and Manchester. In the meantime things were not going too well on the Stockton and Darlington line, largely because Stephenson was rarely there to see to things himself. Much was left to his faithful Timothy Hackworth, who acted as locomotive engineer and did a good deal of experimental work on his own account. Stephenson, for a man of such humble birth, had a highly developed business instinct, and together with his son Robert and some other friends launched a locomotive building business of his own under the name of Robert Stephenson & Co. Ltd. The interest that was being taken in railways in many parts of the world offered promise of a good business in locomotive building; and at that time, despite the set-back on the Stockton and Darlington Railway the 'know-how' of the Stephensons, father and son, was unparalleled.

In the late 1820s, however, and for some little time thereafter, many of those most anxious to have railways were by no means convinced that the haulage should be by steam locomotives. They were not impressed by the possibilities of speedy travel that steam appeared to hold out. While the prospect of getting horse-drawn mail and passenger coaches was welcome enough to many who had to endure the rigours and hazards of travel on the existing highways, it was reliability rather than increased speed that was the main attraction. As to goods, it was seriously proposed that the Liverpool and Manchester Railway should be worked by cable traction, powered by a series of stationary steam engines. Between the rival factions within the Board of the Liverpool and Manchester Railway a great battle was waged: steam locomotives *versus* cable or horse traction. The outcome was that cable traction was decided upon for the severe gradient from Liverpool terminus up to Edge Hill, and steam locomotives for the rest of the line.

George Stephenson was the Engineer of the line, but this did not automatically mean that his son's firm would supply the locomotives. The directors were anxious to throw the competition for the motive power as wide open as possible, so they offered a prize of £500 for the locomotive that should best fulfil certain conditions of haulage. The celebrated Rainhill trials were the result, and the competing engines are illustrated and described later in this book. Certain popular prints of the day show the three principal competitors running abreast in the manner of a horse-race; but no such race actually took place. Each locomotive set about its prescribed task separately under the close observation of impartial witnesses and under the eyes of their rivals, and the results were carefully collated and assessed before any announcement of the 'winner' was made. The triumph of Stephenson's *Rocket* in this competition set the firm off on a career of locomotive-building that took its products into almost every country where there were railways.

In the meantime, great improvements were made in the design of rails. The invention at the Bedlington Iron Works, in Northumberland, of the process of rolling wrought iron rails into far longer lengths than it had previously been possible to cast them, reduced the number of joints in the rails that were required but at that time the most generally satisfactory way of supporting the rails and maintaining them properly in place was to mount them on heavy stone blocks. These were set deeply into the ground at fairly close intervals, and by their very size and weight could be guaranteed to stay put. Unfortunately,

some individual blocks tended to 'settle' more than others, with the result that the track became uneven. Furthermore these huge blocks had little 'give' in them when a train was passing over, so that the riding was harsh and full of constant vibration. Many years were to pass before the ideal form of railway permanent way was evolved, and the illustrated section of the book shows a number of different forms of track that were tried in different parts of the world.

The earliest forms of steam locomotive were of very restricted power, and it was considered necessary in Great Britain and France particularly to keep the new railways as level as possible. George Stephenson himself stated that the maximum gradient for steam traction should not be steeper than 1 in 330. In passing through anything but level plains such railways needed very large engineering works in the form of high embankments, deep cuttings and long tunnels, and some of these works, particularly when high viaducts were needed to cross deep valleys, involved magnificent works of architecture. No less impressive were some of the earlier terminal stations designed by the leading architects of the day. Primitive though much of the rolling stock and fixed equipment was, those who built the earlier railways in many parts of the world sensed that they were engaged on great pioneer works, and the entrances to them, through which travellers passed in their own carriages, were designed to impress. Pictures in later sections of this book show some of the magnificent French, German and American stations, the architecture of which may well have been inspired, in spirit if not in actual style, by the great entrance to the London and Birmingham Railway beneath the Doric Arch at Euston, and the little less impressive classical portico of the original Birmingham terminus at Curzon Street.

The conveyance of passengers was a highly controversial business in many countries. While every consideration was given to the first-class passenger, who had previously travelled inside on the old stage coaches, second- and third-class passengers were less welcome, and the kind of accommodation provided for them was hardly an inducement to travel for pleasure. In England, some politicians of the more reactionary kind regarded railways as something of a menace. Their introduction came at a time of great political unrest, and the great Duke of Wellington for one expressed the gravest concern that *radical* bands could be moved from one part of the country to another to ferment trouble. On the other hand, the railways were prepared to convey the private carriages of wealthy patrons secured on flat trucks, so that such passengers had not the inconvenience of changing from their own carriages to railway vehicles and could travel with their own servants in attendance. For the most part, the early carriages available to the public on European railways were very similar, and in several countries the carrying capacity of individual vehicles was increased by double-decking.

Early development in the U.S.A. tended to follow different lines. It was rather the case of opening up new lines of communication rather than offering a quicker and improved means of transit between long-established centres of population, culture and trade as in Europe. From the outset track began to take a different form. Whereas British, and to a large extent Continental European, railways were established as private property with penal-

ties for trespassing and so on, the American 'right of way', as it was often termed, was unfenced and quite open to the public. Not only this, but the track-laying was less precisely done. The rails were supported on 'ties', as the sleepers are known in America, formed of timbers cut from the forests. Very little shaping was applied to the natural form of the hewn trees, and it was in these circumstances that the Vignoles, or flat-bottomed rail became universally adopted. It was ideally suited to spiking straight down on to the cross-ties. Very little ballasting was applied. Little more was done on many routes than lay the ties on to the natural ground. Cheapness in construction was a notable feature of many of the early American railways, and consummate skill was developed in the art of viaduct construction by timber trestling. In England the great pioneer engineer, Isambard Kingdom Brunel, of the Great Western Railway, used trestle spans for many picturesque viaducts in South Devon and Cornwall; but in the majority of these the trestle spread out fanwise from the tops of massive stone piers. The Americans built their viaducts entirely of timber.

The distinctive nature of American permanent way, and its less stable road-bed led, at an early date, to the development of rolling stock that was distinctive in many ways from that of European countries. While the earliest passenger carriages were four-wheelers, the bogie carriage soon made an appearance. The mounting of relatively long bodies on two pivoted mountings gave easier riding and rendered the vehicles less likely to derailment on the roughly-laid, uneven tracks. Carriages increased in size much more rapidly than in Britain or Continental Europe. On the British railways in particular the majority of the station yards were laid out with small turntables, just large enough to take one four-wheeled carriage. The coaches were light enough to be pushed by hand, and these turntables enabled them to be transferred rapidly from one track to another without the complication of shunting over points or crossovers. With so many of these turntables eventually in existence, and the station yards constructed accordingly, there was naturally reluctance to depart from small four-wheeled coaches that would fit the turntables. The Americans were free from any considerations of this kind and the 'cars' soon became so large as to dwarf the early locomotives.

Station design differed in Great Britain from most parts of the world in two respects. There was, first of all, the height of the platforms. While the very earliest railways were conceived on stage coach lines, and involved passengers climbing into the carriages from ground level, it very soon became the practice in Great Britain to build platforms of such a height that passengers could step level into the carriages. This practice has been followed to no more than a limited extent in Europe. The 'platform areas' are delineated by low platforms, beyond which passengers are not normally permitted to walk, but it is still something of a climb to get into the carriages. Another difference that grew up from quite early days was that of keeping the tracks and platforms quite separate from the main station buildings. The 'operating' part of the stations, in the U.S.A. in particular, is frequently referred to as 'the train shed'. The illustrations in this book include many examples of magnificent station façades in the U.S.A. and in Europe; and in comparing these with British principal stations, the marked segregation of what may be termed the

'operating' and the 'social' side will be particularly noted. In the older English stations, like Kings Cross, Paddington and Liverpool Street in London, social amenities and trains exist cheek by jowl. The earlier Continental stations, of which the *Gare de l'Est* in Paris, and Munich are examples, are in some ways a half-way house between the British and the American form of layout. But whatever the form of layout, the earlier railway stations in all countries formed an important expression of the architectural styles of the day, and from the illustrations in this book it will be seen that many of them were not merely impressive—they were magnificent.

Reverting again to American railways, the most cursory glance through the illustrations is enough to show that some of the early locomotives were of quite extraordinary appearance, and still more extraordinary finish. A railway enthusiast familiar with early British designs, and knowing something of their Continental contemporaries, might well wonder if some of the American locomotives depicted were not the figment of some leg-pulling artist's imagination, rather than of sober fact! But having got beyond its primitive stages there developed a period on the railways in the U.S.A. when locomotives were extraordinarily ornate. As in Great Britain, drivers had their own engines and to the manufacturers' adornments—and they were many!—were added many touches of the driver's own personality. Fancy scrollwork was added to the cab and tender panels and additional items of colour were decked here, there and everywhere. This is not to say that there were locomotives everywhere in the U.S.A. like *S. Meredith*, which is the subject of one of our pictures. It is unfortunate, however, that authentic records of some of the colours have not been preserved. In those early years the individual railways did not have their own specific liveries. The painting of locomotives, as they first went into service at any rate, was largely decided by the manufacturers. What happened afterwards was usually in the hands of the driver, if he happened to be artistically minded.

The matter of manufacturers' painting styles introduces another unique feature of early American railroading. None of the early railways appear to have employed engineers whose task it was to formulate policy. There were no American counterparts of men like Buddicom, Alexander Allan or James Edward McConnell. In the U.S.A. the manufacturers were at first setting the pace, and it was their practice to produce beautifully-executed drawings from which engravings were made. These latter were coloured by hand, and a locomotive builder would go to a railway management and say, in effect, 'How would you like a few locomotives like this?' It is from such of these early engravings that have survived and other collateral information that the colours of some early American locomotives are now known; and it is on the basis of research of this nature that we have been able to show some of the startling locomotives, the goings of which enlivened the early American railways. Their mechanical design, and how they were devised to run successfully on the roughly-laid tracks of 120 to 140 years ago, is discussed in connection with some of the individual engines illustrated. Their general appearance suggests the tales of 'Wells Fargo', and the story of American railways in our period is fittingly wound up by an account of the very exciting episode with the *General* during the Civil War of 1861.

In no respect is the development of early railways more picturesquely shown than in evolution of methods of signalling. The speed of locomotives on the first public railways was strictly regulated, and one of our pictures shows the scene on the opening day of the Stockton and Darlington Railway when the steam-hauled train was preceded by a man riding on a horse. It was when the speed of locomotives began to exceed considerably the maximum speed of horses that some form of signalling became necessary. There were two forms of indication needed. One was akin to the common-or-garden 'traffic-cop' regulating the traffic in station areas, and at various points along the line; and the second was to give advanced notice of a stop required to a train travelling at maximum speed. On some of the early English railways it was the practice to station 'policemen' at certain strategic points. These men were under a kind of military discipline and gave signals by strictly-regulated positions of their arms. Of course these men could be seen only when the train was at close quarters, and for the longer range type of indication various forms of signal were devised. In England nearly all of these gave an indication only when there was danger ahead by red flags hoisted high, or a red ball. The use of a red ball on high was in contrast and opposite in principle to the American use of a ball signal; for in the latter case a 'high ball' was the clear signal. Even today, railway jargon in the U.S.A. speaks of a train 'high-balling' through a station if it is running through at full speed.

The genesis of what became the standard form of mechanical signal on the railways of Great Britain lay in the Admiralty semaphores erected on prominent heights between London and the South Coast when a Napoleonic invasion was expected. These semaphore signals were erected on towers built at intervals so that from any one post the signals to fore and aft could be seen, in daylight at any rate. From this old installation came the idea of the semaphore signal on railways which was so designed as to give three indications: horizontal meant 'stop'; inclined diagonally downwards was 'caution', while the arm hanging vertically down signified 'all-clear'. There was a faulty principle involved in all the early signals mentioned except that of the American 'high-ball'. If the red flag, target or ball was not displayed a driver was justified in assuming he had a clear run. But if the apparatus was broken or had fallen down the 'all clear' could be a false one. It was the same with the earliest application of semaphores to railway signalling. The semaphore worked in a slot in the post, and in the 'all clear' position, when it hung vertically down, it was completely out of sight. The same assurance could quite falsely be given if the arm had broken away from its bearings and fallen to the ground.

When steam was well established as the natural and generally accepted means of power for operating railways, there soon arose inventors who tried to provide 'improved' methods other than steam.

While the first-class passenger had a comfortable if rather constrained ride inside his coachlike compartment, others were not so fortunate, and there were constant complaints about the smoke and smuts thrown out by locomotives and the danger from fire if sparks lodged on the roofs of carriages where it was usual to pile passengers' luggage. One gallant, but unsuccessful attempt to get away from steam traction was the so-called Atmospheric system, first installed in Ireland on the Dublin and Kingstown line. Brunel saw this system at work, and was so convinced of its efficiency that he invested heavily in it, and recommended it for adoption on the broad-gauge line of the South Devon Railway between Exeter and Plymouth. Some of the curious trains and equipment used with this system are illustrated and described; but although it worked very well when new, some parts of the apparatus deteriorated very rapidly, and after a short time it had to be written off as a costly failure. Thus, except on a few short and very steep inclines where rope traction was used, the steam locomotive was left in sole possession everywhere in the world. It remained so to the end of the period covered by this book, and it was only towards the end of the period next in this series, going from 1860 to 1895, that electric traction was first introduced.

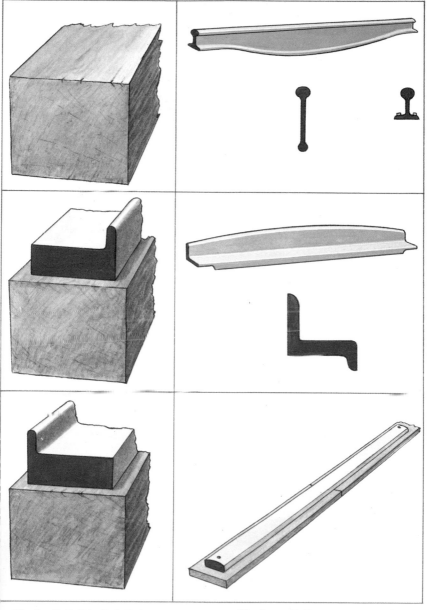

1 **Wooden Rail:** Prior Park, Bath, 1733.
2 **Inside Flange Iron Rail:** Coalbrookdale, 1767.
3 **Outside Flange Iron Rail:** Duke of
   Norfolk's colliery.

4 **The Jessop Rail:** 1789.
5 **Cast Rail:** Surrey Iron Railway, 1803.
6 **Lord Carlisle's Wrought Iron Rail:** 1811.

EVOLUTION OF TRACK IN ENGLAND

7   **Iron Rail on Wooden Blocks.**

8   **Wooden Rail on Cross Sleepers.**

9 **Losh and Stephenson's Scarfed Rail Joints.**

10 **Busselton Incline:** track on stone blocks.

11 **Richard Trevithick's** *Pen-y-darran*, 1804.

12 **Richard Trevithick's** *Catch-me-who-can*, 1808.

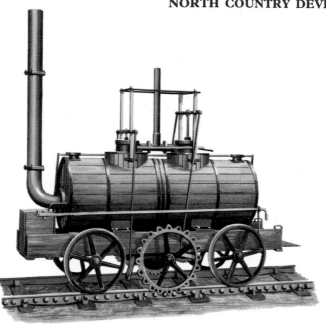

13 **Blenkinsop Locomotive:** 1811.

14 **W. Hedley's** *Puffing Billy*: 1815.

15 **A Typical Chaldron Wagon.**

16 **Horse-drawn Wagon on Plateway.**

17 Horse-traction in Collieries.

18 A Dandy Car, with its Passenger.

19 **Hetton Colliery Locomotive 1822:** the driver.

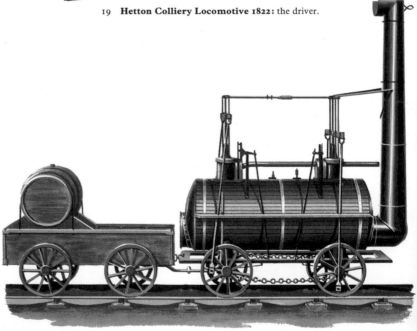

20 **The Killingworth Type of Locomotive.**

21 **A Rear-end View of** *Puffing Billy*.

22 **Stockton & Darlington Railway:** a horse-drawn coach.

23 **Stockton & Darlington Railway:** coach interior.

24 **Stockton & Darlington Railway:** precautions with steam, the red flag leads.

25 **Stockton & Darlington Railway:** the *Locomotion*, 1825.

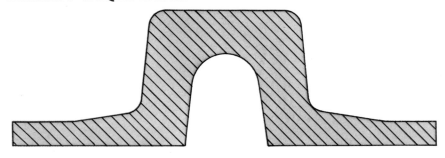

26 **Brunel's Broad-Gauge Permanent Way:** the rail section.

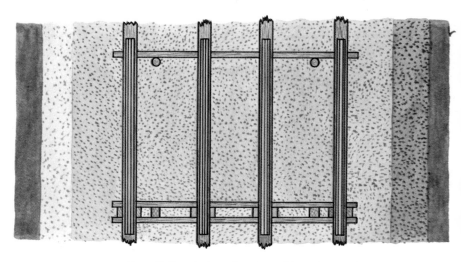

27 **Brunel's Broad-Gauge Permanent Way:** plan of double-track.

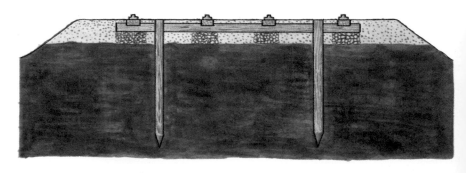

28 **Brunel's Broad-Gauge Permanent Way:** cross-section of double-track.

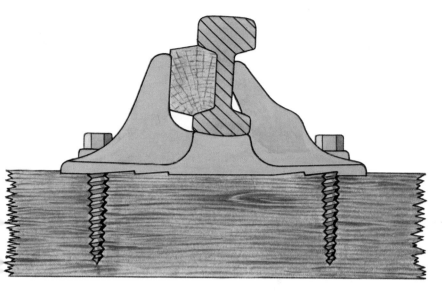

29　**Section of Bull Head Type of Rail,** as later developed.

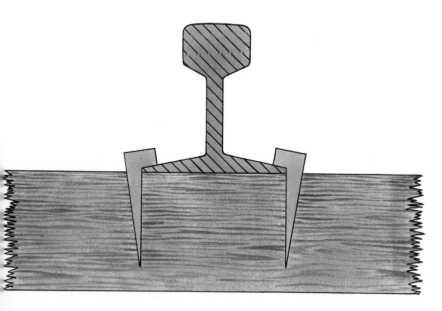

30　**Section of Flat-bottomed, or Vignoles Rail.**

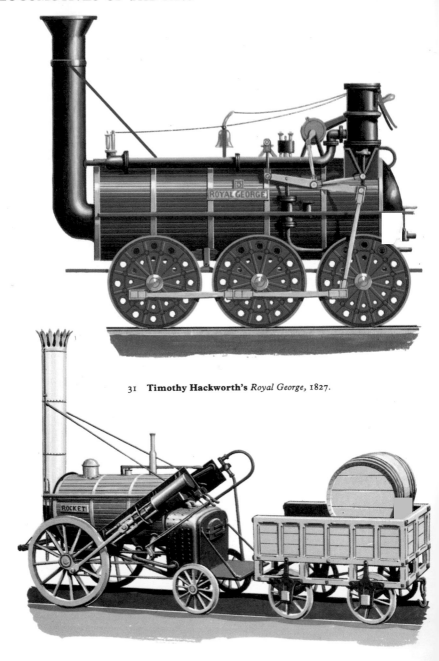

31 **Timothy Hackworth's** *Royal George*, 1827.

32 **Rainhill Competitors 1:** Robert Stephenson's *Rocket*.

33 **Rainhill Competitors 2:** Timothy Hackworth's *Sansparail*

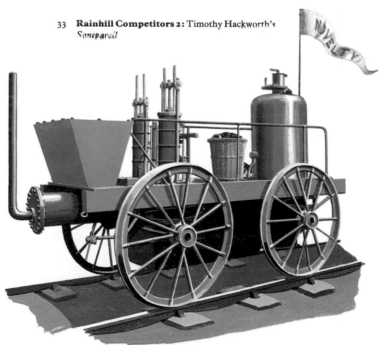

34 **Rainhill Competitors 3:** Ericsson & Braithwaite's *Novelty*.

35 **Liverpool & Manchester Railway:** the Moorish Arch.

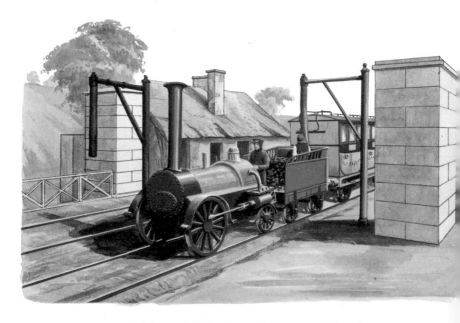

36 **Liverpool & Manchester Railway:** a wayside station.

37 **London & Birmingham Railway**: the Doric Arch, Euston.

38 **London & Birmingham Railway:** Curzon Street Station,
Birmingham.

39   **Liverpool & Manchester Railway:** mail coach.

40   **Liverpool & Manchester Railway:** third-class carriage.

41　**Liverpool & Manchester Railway:** livestock van with drovers.

42　**Liverpool & Manchester Railway:** a double-decked sheep van.

43 **Mohawk & Hudson Railroad:** the *De Witt Clinton*, 1831.

44 **Mohawk & Hudson Railroad:** a first-class carriage.

45 **Baltimore & Ohio Railroad:** the Imlay carriage.

46 **Camden & Amboy Railroad:** an early bogie coach.

47 **St. Etienne & Andrezieux Railway:** passenger train haulage.

48 **St. Etienne & Andrezieux Railway:** double-decker passenger coach.

BELGIUM

49 **Brussels & Malines Railway:** passenger coach.

ENGLAND

50 **Stockton & Darlington Railway:** closed-in passenger coach.

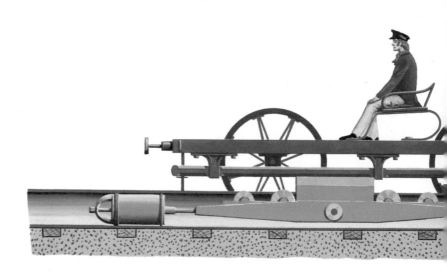

51　**Atmospheric System:** the traction unit.

52.　**Atmospheric System:** cross-section of traction unit.

53 **Atmospheric System:** pumping station at Dawlish.

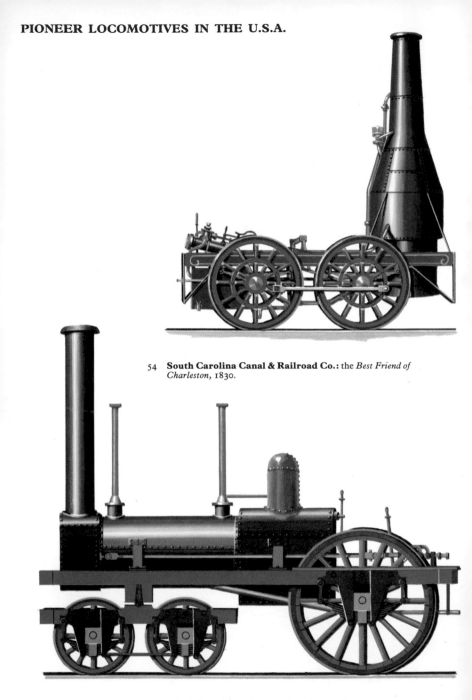

54 **South Carolina Canal & Railroad Co.:** the *Best Friend of Charleston*, 1830.

55 **West Point Foundry:** the *Experiment*, 1832.

56 **Baltimore & Ohio Railroad:** the *Lafayette*, 1837, a Norris
'One-Armed Billy',

57 **Stockton & Darlington Railway:** the *Wilberforce*, 1831.

58   **The Admiralty Semaphores.**

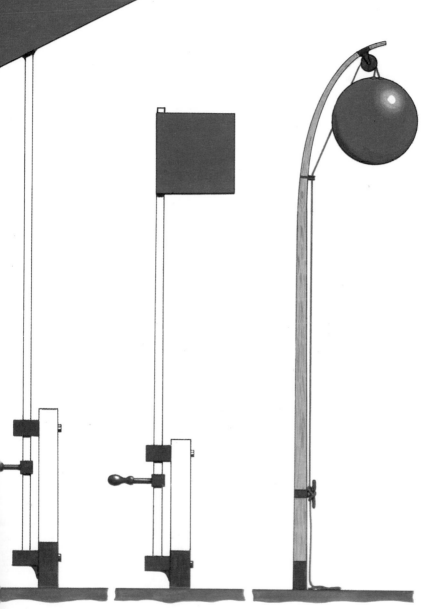

59–61 **Primitive Forms of Railway Warning Signals.**

DEVELOPING CARRIAGE STYLES

FRANCE

62 **Paris & St. Germain Railway:** first-class carriage.

ENGLAND

63 **Newcastle & South Shields Railway:** passenger carriage.

64–65 **French Railways:** a road-railer carriage, shown in the road and rail travelling positions.

EVOLVING STEAM LOCOMOTIVE DESIGN

GERMANY

66   **The First Steam Locomotive in Germany:** *Der Adler*.

ENGLAND

67   **Stockton & Darlington Railway:** 2–2–0 locomotive,
Sunbeam.

68 **Liverpool & Manchester Railway:** a Bury 0 4 0, the *Liverpool,*

69 **Dublin & Kingstown Railway:** a Forrester 2–2–0, the *Vauxhall.*

70 **Liverpool & Manchester Railway:** the *Lion*.

71 **Newcastle & Carlisle Railway:** the 0–4–0 *Lightning*.

72 **Marietta & Cincinatti Railroad:** the 4–4–0 *Washington*

73 **Paterson & Ramapo Railroad:** the 4–4–0 *Ramapo*.

FOUR-WHEELED CARRIAGES

ENGLAND

74 **Newcastle & Carlisle Railway:** first-class carriage, late 1830s.

75 **Newcastle & Carlisle Railway:** second-class carriage, late 1830s.

76 **An Italian Second-class Carriage:** 1840.

77 **Bodmin & Wadebridge Railway, Cornwall:** a composite carriage, 1838.

BUILDING OF THE LONDON & BIRMINGHAM

78 **London & Birmingham Railway:** building the Boxmoor embankment.

79 **London & Birmingham Railway:** a handsome underline bridge near Rugby.

80 **London & Birmingham Railway:** building the great
Kilsby Tunnel.

LOCOMOTIVES: CONVENTIONAL AND FREAK

ENGLAND

81　**Great Western Railway:** experimental express passenger
locomotive, *Hurricane*, 1838.

ENGLAND

82　**Newcastle & Carlisle Railway:** 0–6–0 goods locomotive,
Newcastle.

83 **First Steam Locomotive built in Belgium:** *Le Belge,*
1835.

RAILWAY STATION ARCHITECTURE

ENGLAND

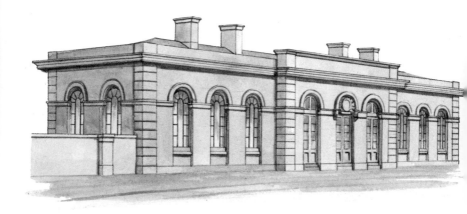

84 **North Midland Railway:** Belper, an early English station.

U.S.A.

85 **Syracuse & Utica Railroad:** Syracuse, an early American station.

86　**Leipzig, Germany:** the first Thuringian station.

87　**Kassel, Germany:** the 'train shed'.

ENGLAND

88 **Great Western Railway:** the *Ajax* locomotive, 1838.

FRANCE

89 **Northern Railway of France:** a Stephenson long-boilered locomotive.

90 **Eastern Counties Railway:** an 0–4–2 saddle tank engine.

91 **Western Railway of France:** a Buddicom 2–2–2 tank engine.

92 **Great Western Railway:** an early Brunel timber trestle bridge.

93 **Great Western Railway:** the skew bridge at Bath.

94   **Great Western Railway:** Box Tunnel.

95   **Great Western Railway:** Teignmouth Tunnel.

GRADUAL DEVELOPMENT OF LOCOMOTIVES

GERMANY

96 **Berlin & Anhalt Railway:** the first Borsig locomotive, 1841.

ENGLAND

97 **Shrewsbury & Chester Railway:** Stephenson's long-boilered 2–4–0 locomotive, 1846.

98 **Henschell & Sohn's First Locomotive:** *Drache*, 1848.

99 **Paris & Versailles Railway:** a standard Stephenson 2–4–0.

100   **York & North Midland Railway:** third-class carriage.

101   **Grand Junction Railway:** Travelling Post Office, 1838.

102 **Great Western Railway:** a third-class, broad-gauge
'Parliamentary' coach.

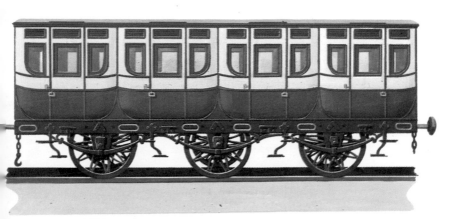

103 **Great Western Railway:** a broad-gauge composite
carriage.

CLASSIC STATION ARCHITECTURE

ENGLAND

104 **London Bridge Station:** exterior.

U.S.A.

105 **Boston, Massachusetts:** The Haymarket station.

106   **Boston & Maine Railroad:** Salem station.

107   **Paris:** the *Gare de l'Est*.

LOCOMOTIVES: THE DEVELOPING TRENDS

AUSTRIA

108 **A Norris Export to Austria:** the *Philadelphia*, 1838.

FRANCE

109 **Northern Railway of France:** a 2–2–2 passenger locomotive.

110   **A Borsig standard 2–2–2.**

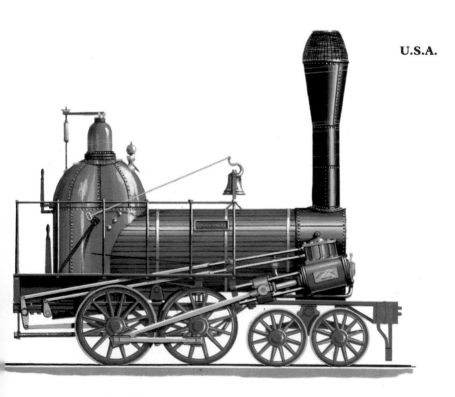

111   **Philadelphia & Reading Railroad:** the 4–4–0 *Gowan and Marx*, 1839.

MOTIVE POWER: CONTINUING DIVERSITY

ENGLAND

112   **Eastern Counties Railway:** Auto-Train, 1849.

U.S.A.

113   **New York & Erie Railway:** a six-foot gauge 4–4–0.

114 **Belgian State Railways:** the 2–4–0 *L'Elephant*.

115 **Early Methods of Signalling:** the 'Policeman'.

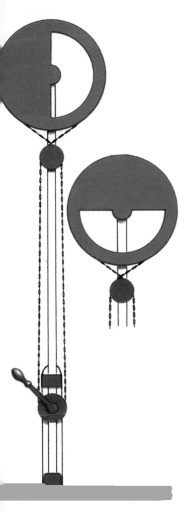

London & South Western Railway: early signals.

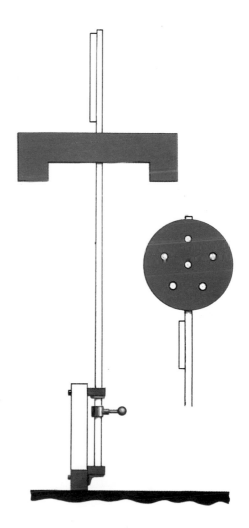

Great Western Railway: Brunel's Disc and Crossbar signal.

A GREAT ENSEMBLE

118 Newcastle Central Station.

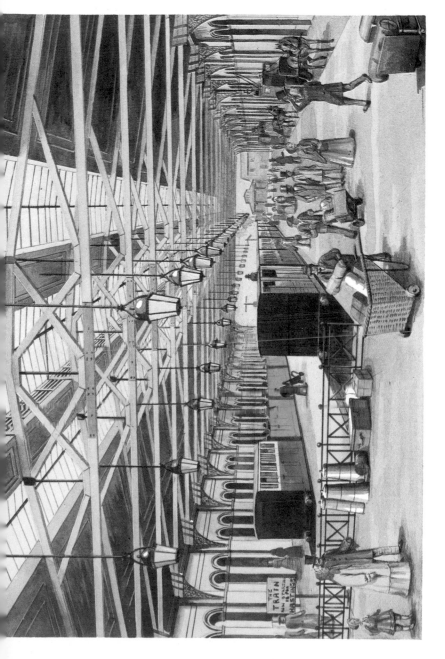

119   **London Bridge Station**: interior, South-Eastern section.

120 **Robert Stephenson's Britannia Tubular Bridge.**

121 **Sculptured Lions for the Britannia Bridge.**

122　**Robert Stephenson's Conway Tubular Bridge:**
capstan in operation.

123　**Conway Bridge and Entrances.**

124 **Gooch's 'Colossal Locomotive':** the *Great Western*.

125 **London & North Western Railway:** the 4–2–2 *Cornwall*, 1847.

126 **Stockton & Darlington Railway:** the 2–2–2 *Meteor*, 1843.

127 **London & North Western Railway, Southern Division:**
Stephenson's long-boilered 4–2–0.

THE PICTURESQUE CRAMPTON TYPE

BELGIUM

128 **Belgium:** the Crampton, *Namur*.

ENGLAND

129 **Eastern Counties Railway:** a Crampton.

130   **Paris, Lyons & Mediterranean Railway: a Crampton.**

131   **Baden State Railway:** the Crampton, *Bardenia*.

132 **Manchester & Leeds Railway:** early second-class carriage.

133 **London & North Western Railway:** passengers' luggage van.

134   **A 'Race Special', 1846:** first-class passengers.

135   **A 'Race Special', 1846:** third-class travel.

MORE PIONEER LOCOMOTIVES

DENMARK

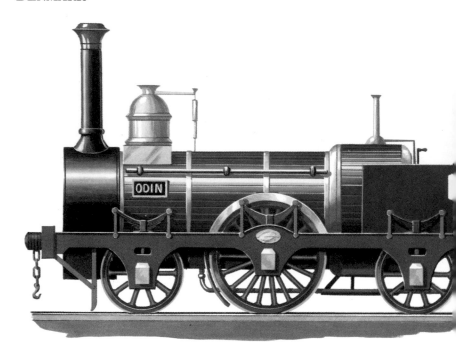

136   **The First Locomotive in Denmark:** *Odin*, 1847.

NORTHERN
ENGLAND

137   **Lancashire & Yorkshire Railway:** an 0–4–2 Bury engine, *Victoria.*

138 **The First Railway in Russia:** a Stephenson 2–2–2 of
      1836.

139 **Eastern Counties Railway:** a Braithwaite 0–4–0.

CLASSIC MAJOR VIADUCTS

ANGLO-SCOTTISH BORDER

140 **The Royal Border Bridge:** Berwick-upon-Tweed.

BRITTANY

141 **A Notable French Viaduct:** Morlaix, on the Le Mans-Brest line.

142   **North Midland Railway:** Milford Tunnel.

143   **Newcastle & Carlisle Railway:** Scotswood Viaduct.

144　**Stockton & Darlington Railway:** Skerne Bridge.

145　**The First Iron Railway Bridge:** Gaunless Valley, near
Bishop Auckland.

146 **Great Western Railway:** the 'Long Charley' carriages.

147 **Carriage Truck for Conveyance of Private Owners' Vehicles.**

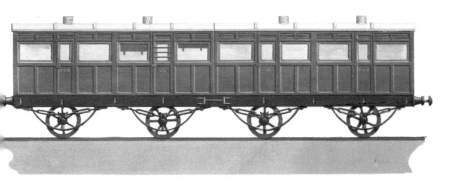

148 **Eastern Counties Railway:** a jointed eight-wheeled carriage, 1847.

149 **London & Birmingham Railway:** a bed carriage.

CONTRASTS IN STATION STYLES

U.S.A.

150   **An Early American Station, 1835:** Lowell.

U.S.A.

151   **An Early American Station, 1850:** Harrisburg, Pennsylvania.

152 **Munich**: the *Hauptbahnhof*.

153 **Brighton Station**: exterior, 1840.

U.S.A.

154 **Baltimore & Ohio Railroad:** a Ross-Winans 'mud-digger' locomotive.

U.S.A.

155 **A Baldwin 'Eight-coupled' Locomotive:** 1846.

156 **Egyptian Government Railways:** a 2–2–? 0﹏﹏
locomotive.

157 **Philadelphia & Reading Railroad:** a Winans 0–8–0,
1846.

VIOLENT CONTRASTS IN CARRIAGES

ENGLAND

158　A Vale-of-Neath Third-class Carriage.

ENGLAND

159　A Bodmin & Wadebridge Second-class Carriage.

160 **Stockton & Darlington Railway:** a composite carriage, 1846.

161 **An Early American Bogie Passenger Car.**

CONTRASTS IN LOCOMOTIVE ADORNMENT

U.S.A.

162   **Rogers, Ketchum & Grosvenor:** a 4–4–0 locomotive.

ENGLAND

163   **London & North Western Railway:** an Allan 2–2–2, the *Menai.*

164 **Shrewsbury & Chester Railway:** a Sharp 2–2–2, 1848.

165 **Cincinatti & Chicago Air Line Railroad:** the 4–4–0
S. Meredith.

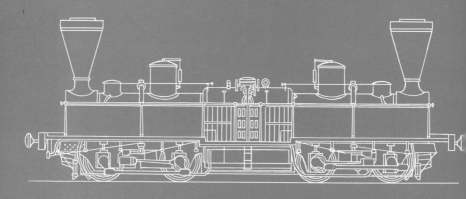

166   **Semmering Trial Contestants:** the *Seraing*.

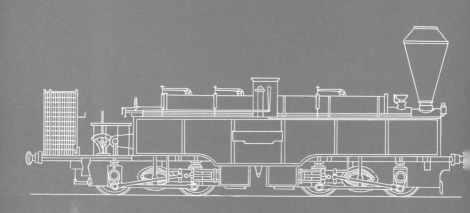

167   **Semmering Trial Contestants:** the *Wiener Neustadt*.

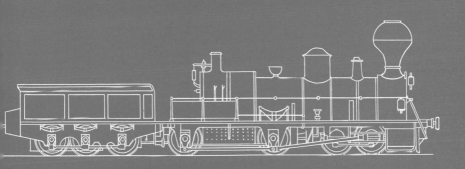

168 **Semmering Trial Contestants:** the *Bavaria*.

169 **Semmering Trial Contestants:** the *Vindobona*.

ENGLAND

ENGLAND   170   **South Eastern Railway:** Shakespeare's Cliff Tunnel.

171   **North Eastern Railway:** Selby Bridge.

172 **Leeds Northern Railway:** Bramhope Tunnel,

173 **Eastern Railway of France:** viaduct at Chaumont.

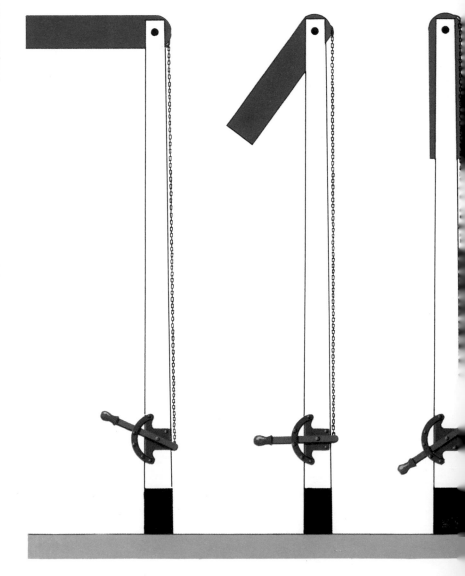

174   Early Semaphore Signals.

175 The American 'Highball' signal.

176 **Great Western Railway:** the 4–2–2 *Iron Duke*, 1847, 'Lord of the Isles' class.

177 **David Joy's Masterpiece:** the 2–2–2 *Jenny Lind.*

178   Western Railway of France: *L'Aigle*.

PIONEER
SWISS

179   Locomotive of the First Swiss Railway: 1847.

ENGLISH INFLUENCE 'DOWN UNDER'

MCCONNELL IN ENGLAND

180 **London & North Western Railway:** a Southern Division
McConnell 0–6–0.

MCCONNELL IN NEW SOUTH WALES

181 **New South Wales Government Railways:** the first
steam locomotive.

182 **London & North Western Railway:** the 2–2–2 *Watt*, 'Lady of the Lake' class.

'CAPTURED BY THE ENEMY'

183 **Western & Atlantic Railroad:** the *General*.

AN IMPOSING AMERICAN STATION

THE DAWN OF
WORLD RAILWAYS 1800–1850

1–6 The Genesis of Railways

The origin of railways can be traced back more than 400 years. Mining is an ancient human craft, and those engaged in it found that heavier loads could be moved by men and animals if the little trucks ran on smooth, prepared paths instead of rough tracks on plain ground. There is a record as far back as the year 1530 of small trucks running on wooden rails at a mine in the Austrian Tyrol. This was a somewhat diminutive affair with a gauge of about 2 ft.; but it was a *railway*, of a kind: Several instances have been traced of the existence of rail, or tramways in England during the sixteenth century and, in connection with coal-mining in the Midlands about the end of that century, it seems probable that there was a railway track in one area for conveying coal to the River Trent. How the wheels were guided on these tracks seems a little obscure, because it was not until the year 1733 that definite proof of the use of a *flanged wooden* wheel is available in the records of the wagonway constructed by the great industrial magnate, Ralph Allen, to convey stone from the quarries beside his mansion, Prior Park, Bath, to the River Avon.

Our first picture, Plate 1, shows Ralph Allen's rail which was of oak measuring 5 in. wide by 5 in. deep. The hard usage to which some of these wooden wagonways were subjected led to heavy wear, and not infrequent breakages, and to improve the operation various forms of iron plating were devised. The techniques becoming available for 'forming' cast iron suggested that the guiding influence could be provided by the rail itself, thus avoiding the expensive alternative of constructing wooden wheels with flanges, and Plate 2 shows a form of rail used at the Coalbrookdale ironworks in 1767. The flange of the rail was on the inside of the wheel, and the trucks were trundled along on the flat, cast-iron surface, and prevented from straying from their proper path by the inside flange. The width of the flat, or running surface, was 4 in. There were, of course, people who wished to do things differently from the pioneers even at that early date and at a colliery near Sheffield, owned by the Duke of Norfolk, the rails were arranged with the flanges outside, as shown in Plate 3; the dimensions of the actual cast-iron section were much the same.

Up to this period a continuous rail of timber had formed the foundation of all railways, whether they had iron running-plates or not; but in 1789 William Jessop patented an entirely new form of rail. It was designed for use with flanged wheels, and it eliminated entirely the use of timber. It consisted of lengths of specially shaped cast iron, about 2 ft. 6 in. long, supported only at the ends and on massive stone blocks. The form of rail is shown in Plate 4, which also includes the cross-sections at the middle and at the ends. The ends had a flat base to facilitate mounting on the stone blocks while the centre part was deep to provide the requisite strength for the unsupported section. The use of flanged wheels was still exceptional rather than general at the end of the eighteenth century, and on the Surrey Iron Railway, in 1803, the rails were a combination of Jessop's unsupported type resting on stone block, with the outside flange of the Duke of Norfolk's Sheffield colliery, Plate 3. This form of rail on the Surrey Iron Railway is shown in Plate 5. A final form of the composite wood and iron rail, dating from 1811 is shown in Plate 6. This was used in some collieries owned by Lord Carlisle, and is interesting as being one of the earliest uses of a wrought-iron, as distinct from a cast-iron, rail.

7–8 Supporting the Rails.

In the early days of wagonways when the speed of running—pulled by horses, or pushed by men—was slow, the foundations of the track were not of very great importance. The main thing was to get a relatively smooth surface, and if the track itself had some incidental undulating parts, due to slight subsidence of the foundation, it did not matter very much. Plates 7 and 8 show two methods of supporting the rails. The first of these includes the Jessop type of rail, but it is supported at the ends by massive wooden blocks sunk to a considerable depth into the ground. Extraordinary though it may seem to us in an era when railway trains run at speeds of 100 m.p.h., or more, the positioning of these blocks in the native earth was the only means to maintain correct guage between the two rails. There appears to have been no packing, or other reinforcement, around the blocks. The second picture, Plate 8, shows an early form of all-timber construction that bears a remarkable resemblance, in a very primitive form, to our modern standard track. The wooden rails are carried slightly above ground level, and secured to cross-ties, or sleepers as we now

call them, at fairly frequent intervals. The sleepers are of roughly the same cross-section as the rails themselves. The rails are of a length to cover two sleeper spacings, and the joints in the rails are staggered. The joints in the left-hand rail are made on the sleeper that is an intermediate support for the right-hand rails, and vice versa. This practice of staggering the rail joints became standard on certain Irish railways in the heyday of the steam era, but it was not adopted in Great Britain.

9–10 The Rails of Losh and Stephenson.

George Stephenson's early experiments with steam locomotives in the first decades of the nineteenth century were made on the rough tracks in the colliery yards of Northumberland, and quite apart from anything he learned about the potentialities of steam and how to use it for traction, he realized that the quality of the tracks would have to be much improved to carry the locomotives he was building. These, of course, were neither very large, nor very heavy; but they were a great deal heavier than the horse-drawn wagons that the colliery rails had had formerly to bear, and there were 'dynamic', as well as dead loads to be considered. Then, as ever since on railways all over the world, the rail joint was a great problem. One has only got to take a glance at the pictures in Plates 7 and 8, and reflect upon the way the simplest joints of that kind deteriorate, to appreciate how such joints would fail under the repeated passage of heavy wagons, let alone the occasional locomotive. George Stephenson was an 'all-rounder' so far as railways were concerned, and in consultation with his friend, William Losh, he patented the form of cast-iron rail shown in Plate 9. The adjacent ends of two cast-iron rails were tapered, mated together in a 'chair' and overlapped for about $2\frac{1}{2}$ in. A bolt was then passed through both flanges of the chair and both rails.

This ingenious arrangement, as will be seen from the picture, provided a continuity of surface in the rail head, and avoided the definite break existing in previous designs. It also put both rail ends in a common support and in the 'chair' provided the first step towards what became the standard form of British permanent way for more than 100 years. In the mining and quarrying districts of England, where the early development of railways was most marked, stone was plentiful, and massive stone block sunk deep into the ground provided the simplest and cheapest form of foundation for the earliest railways. When the Liverpool and Manchester Railway was built in the late 1820s these stone blocks cost a mere 1s. 4d. each, and the cast-iron chairs in which the rails rested cost almost exactly the same. In fixing the chairs to the stone blocks Stephenson used an equivalent of the modern 'Rawlplug', drilling the stone, and inserting a wooden plug into which the spike for the chair could be driven. The great trouble with the stone blocks, so far as the developing railways were concerned, was that it was very difficult to maintain what modern permanent-way men call 'a good top'. The odd block would sink slightly into the ground, and at once there would be irregularities in the line and level of the rails. Plate 10 shows a typical piece of stone block track, with the Losh and Stephenson type of chair and rail joint, as used on one of the old colliery lines in County Durham—part, in fact, of the purely mineral section of the Stockton and Darlington Railway. The stone block

form of construction lasted until the early 1830s after which the rapid increase in speed led to evolution on different lines that will be described later in this book.

11–12 The Locomotives of Richard Trevithick:
(The *Pen-y-darran* and the *Catch-me-who-can*.)

Although the inception of railways as a means of conveyance for the general public will always be credited, and rightly so, to George Stephenson, the development of the locomotive itself goes back more than twenty years before the opening of the Stockton and Darlington Railway, and the great Cornish engineer Richard Trevithick can be claimed as the undisputed father of the locomotive. But Trevithick was not an 'all-rounder' like Stephenson; he was a dashing adventurer, a pioneer, who having got so far with one invention would be lured away into new channels. Consequently he never followed up, and never reaped the reward of his astonishing pioneer work. It was typical of his whole life that the ever-famous *Pen-y-darran* locomotive should have made its inaugural run as a result of a heavy wager between Samuel Homfray, the South Wales Ironmaster, and Anthony Hill of the Plymouth ironworks. The task was for Trevithick's pioneer locomotive to haul a load of ten tons of iron on the plateway from Pen-y-darran to Abercynon Basin on the Glamorganshire Canal, $9\frac{3}{4}$ miles. Hill bet Homfray 500 guineas even money it couldn't be done. There was tremendous excitement in the neighbourhood. Trevithick revelled in the sporting atmosphere, and just before the trial was writing to one of his Cornish friends to say that the engine was doing so well that he thought they could do the job with 40 tons hung on behind, let alone 10 tons! The trial took place on 21 February 1804 and then the load was 10 tons of iron, 5 wagons and 70 men riding on them. They made the journey from end to end in 4 hours 5 minutes, but this included some stops—not to fettle up the locomotive, but to cut down some obstructing trees, and remove large rocks from the track. Samuel Homfray won his bet all right, and the result was a triumph for Trevithick. But the locomotive left a trail of destruction in her wake. A large number of the rails in the plateway were broken by the weight of the locomotive. Trevithick then ran his *Catch-me-who-can* round a circular enclosed track in London (see Plate 12); but the most sensational development was that Trevithick was preparing to run one of his locomotives 'against any horse, mare, or gelding that may be produced' at the October 1808 race-meeting at Newmarket. The race between the locomotive and horse never took place, although on the preliminary betting it was evident that the *Catch-me-who-can* was the favourite! But after this Trevithick dropped completely out of the picture and it was left to his son Francis, and one of his grandsons in Egypt, to advance the art of locomotive engineering.

13 Blenkinsop Locomotive, 1811.

The locomotives built by Richard Trevithick played havoc with the primitive plateways on which they ran, and those who watched them at work detected what they thought was a certain amount of wheel-slip. They attributed this as much to the use of smooth wheels running on smooth rails as to the light quality of the tracks. It was thought that in order to pull

heavy loads, or to ascend even a moderate gradient, it would be necessary to drive through a geared wheel working in a rack fixed on the track. The Blenkinsop locomotive built on this principle, and illustrated here was designed for a wagonway running from Middleton to the outskirt of Leeds. This engine, weighing 5 tons, is reported to have hauled a load of 90 tons at 4 m.p.h. on level track, and to have conveyed a load of 15 tons up a gradient of 1 in 20. It was a cumbersome and expensive affair, and heavy wear took place between the driving gear wheel and the horizontal rack. But in another respect Blenkinsop's engine marked an important step forward Trevithick's locomotives each had only one cylinder, and had necessarily large flywheels to carry the motion over dead centre. Blenkinsop used two cylinders working alternately on the same shaft.

14 W. Hedley's *Puffing Billy*, 1815.

The work of Blenkinsop had been very closely watched by the engineer of Wylam Colliery, Blackett by name, and in conjunction with his mechanical inspector W. Hedley, he carried out a number of experiments on the adhesion between wheel and rail. At Wylam it was felt that the elaborate gearing of Blenkinsop was not really necessary, and the outcome of much experimenting was the very famous Hedley locomotive, *Puffing Billy*, built in 1815. Like Blenkinsop the Wylam engine had two cylinders, driving through an elaborate system of linkage on the top of the boiler, and then transmitting the power to the wheels through a chain of gear wheels, at axle level. The gear mechanism divided the drive between two axles and by this distribution of the thrust from the pistons halved the driving torque on the main axles, and so lessened the chance of wheel slip. Although it had many imperfections, and apparently did not steam very well, the *Puffing Billy* marked another step forward in that the practicability of using smooth wheels on smooth rails was satisfactorily demonstrated. (*See also* Plate 21.)

15–18 Wagons and Horses.

While it was the invention of the locomotive that gave such a tremendous fillip to the projecting of railways in many parts of England, it must be borne in mind that by the time the pioneer locomotives of Blenkinsop and Hedley were at work there were many private railways, or wagonways operated entirely by horses. In many ways, the geography of the counties of Durham and Northumberland favoured the use of horses. The loaded trains of coal made their ways to the nearest seaport on favourable gradients, and much of the journey could be made under the influence of gravity alone. It was however necessary to provide balanced workings—to use a modern term—for the source of motive power, and so provision had to be made for the horse to travel in the train when the running was under the action of gravity. But before coming to the special provision made for the horses the ordinary wagons must be mentioned.

The wagons in use for colliery railways were, generally speaking, of two types: the primitive open box, or tub (Plate 16), and the chaldron type, which had a tapered body, and which was suitable for tipping out the contents at the appropriate place. When the Stockton and Darlington Railway was opened in 1825, its wagon stock was entirely of this latter type, and it was amusing to recall that these wagons were

at times used indiscriminately for freight and passengers. Even on so auspicious an occasion as the public opening of the railway, the special train included only one coach designed exclusively for passengers and this conveyed only the directors and shareholders. It is amusing to read that the special train included five wagons laden with coal and passengers; one wagon laden with flour and passengers; six wagons with strangers seated; fourteen wagons with workmen and others standing; and six wagons laden with coals. How the passengers and coals were loaded into the same wagon is not explained!

However indiscriminately the chaldron wagons were used for passengers and merchandise one thing is certain: they could not carry horses! The job of carrying sheep and cattle by railway had not been thought of when the Stockton and Darlington Railway was built, and so special vehicles were designed (Plate 18) for horses when they were detached from trains travelling down inclines by gravity. Each of the coal trains had one of these so-called 'dandy-carts' marshalled at the rear end. The horses very quickly got to know the points at which their work temporarily ceased, and once unhitched they could scarcely wait to get to the rear end of the train and climb up into the dandy. A contemporary account tells of how one horse 'fairly laughed' again with pleasure at getting into the cart, in anticipation of its ride down the incline. One of these dandy-carts, with a dummy horse, is preserved in the railway museum at York. At a slightly later period the term 'dandy' became attached to any railway vehicle that was drawn by a horse, rather than applied to something in which the horse itself rode. In a former volume of this series, *Railways in the Years of Pre-Eminence 1905–19*, the celebrated Port Carlisle *Dandy* is illustrated and described. This was a passenger vehicle, rather like an old-style 'toast-rack' tram-car, drawn by a single horse. On the Stockton and Darlington Railway, reliance was placed upon horse traction for many years. At the time of the public opening in 1825 the company had only one steam locomotive, and that was not very reliable. In fact, the overall performance of steam locomotives in the early days of the railway was so erratic as to suggest to many people that horses were after all better, and that future railways should be planned for horse-traction only.

19–20 The Hetton and Killingworth Locomotives

In referring to the locomotives of the Stockton and Darlington Railway in the previous paragraphs, we had drawn a little ahead of strict chronological order, because before George Stephenson built *Locomotion* No. 1, Plate 25, some developments in the evolution of the British steam railway locomotive took place. Stephenson's straight-forward and genial personality made him many friends and of these there was, at that time in his career, no one more important than Nicholas Wood, at Killingworth Colliery. The talents of Wood and Stephenson were complementary to each other. Wood was the scientist with a sound theoretical background, while Stephenson was the eminent practical mechanic who had an astonishing flair for *making* things go. Their friendship and partnership was very fruitful, and it was during those formative years at Killingworth that many problems fundamental to the working of steam locomotives were ironed out. It was during this period that Stephenson, in his natural

inclination to make things as simple as possible, attached the connecting-rods from the pistons direct to crank-pins on the wheels, and thus avoided all the complicated and expensive gearing on the *Puffing Billy*. The Killingworth engine, Plate 20, drew a load of 20 tons at 4 m.p.h. up a slight gradient of 1 in 450.

Puffing Billy derived its name from the sound made by the exhaust steam, but the exhaust became a matter of embarrassment to Stephenson on the Killingworth Colliery railway. The steam was exhausted direct from the cylinder ends, and made a sharp hissing noise. The noise was occasionally simulated by more modern locomotives when starting up with the cylinder cocks open to clear any condensation that might have collected while the engine was standing. But it is one thing to have a brief 'hissing' in the neighbourhood of large stations under strictly controlled modern conditions, but quite another to go trundling through the rural countryside of more than a hundred years ago, doing it all the way. Cattle took fright and stampeded; chickens and ducks panicked and the farming community threatened Stephenson with an injunction! He overcame it in a very simple way, by leading the exhaust from the cylinders so that it passed through the smokebox and up the chimney. This acted not only as a very effective silencer, but the exhaust provided an additional draught on the fire and improved the steaming. In this latter respect the Killingworth engines as developed by George Stephenson were a great advance upon Hedley's *Puffing Billy*, which in its original form steamed poorly. The practice of turning the exhaust from the cylinders up the chimney led, some ten years later, to a great controversy between Stephenson and Timothy Hackworth, who became foreman of locomotives on the Stockton and Darlington Railway when Stephenson himself was away, busy with other projects. But in the years 1815-22 Stephenson had progressed a long way towards producing a reliable slow-speed mineral traffic locomotive.

One of his locomotives, built for the Hetton Colliery railway in 1822, and embodying all the latest Killingworth practice, was shown in rebuilt form at the Railway Centenary celebration pageant at Darlington in 1925. This locomotive was tended by a driver in contemporary costume (Plate 19) and the idea of enginemen clad in white trousers certainly excites the imagination today. However 'rough and tumble' the conditions might be on the private colliery railways of Northumberland and Durham, when it came to providing a public service the drivers had to be attired at least as smartly as the drivers and guards of the stage coaches. There is little doubt that white trousers did not last long as a workaday attire, and some of the earliest photographs of actual locomotives and their crews show tough, deeply-bronzed characters on the footplate, clad in 'sensible clothes', suitable to the open cabs of the day, when smoke and smuts, no less than wind and sunshine, contributed to their complexions. Our picture of the Hetton Colliery locomotive gives a vivid impression of the complicated ironmongery carried outside on these early locomotives, and to see it all in action— beams rising and falling, others slowly oscillating—was to leave one completely fascinated.

21 A Rear-End View of *Puffing Billy*.

Before leaving the 1810-20 decade it is necessary to take another look at *Puffing Billy* and this time from the driver's end. This view, which incidentally emphasizes the rather rough construction of these pioneer locomotives, appears to indicate that there was no fire-hole door. The picture shows the second state of the engine. As first built in 1815 it would not steam, and in less than a year Hedley had to think again and produce a different type of boiler. He got over the difficulty by putting in a return flue in the boiler, but this involved another problem. The return flue meant that the firehole door had got to be at the same end as the chimney, and in consequence of this neither could be on the longitudinal centre-line of the locomotive. Our picture shows how the chimney had to be mounted to one side. If one took a view of the opposite end of the locomotive the firehole door was on the left-hand side and the chimney on the right. This meant that the tender containing the coal and the fireman had to be attached ahead of the locomotive, and driver and fireman were at opposite ends of the boiler. As will be told later this became common practice on some of the early railways in the north-east of England, though George Stephenson himself never adopted it. (See also Plate 14.)

22-23 Stockton and Darlington Railway: A Horse-Drawn Coach.

As the first *public* railway in the world, the Stockton and Darlington assumed special responsibilities that had not to be shouldered by the purely private railways laid in collieries and for local industrial purposes. Passengers may have been carried, at the price of a tip to the driver, or for some other consideration; but the Stockton and Darlington was in public business, authorised by Act of Parliament, and under the eye of the Board of Trade. Nevertheless it is evident that passengers were a secondary consideration. The original horse-drawn coaches were operated by licensed contractors. The closed-in carriages were of the stage-coach type, and the fares were $1\frac{1}{2}d.$ a mile 'inside' and $1d.$ a mile 'outside'. The general 'set out' was very much on stage-coach lines with scarlet-coated drivers and guards. Of course it was a case of one coach, one horse. There was no question of a horse pulling a train of coaches. The construction of the line, with the rails mounted on stone blocks was ideal for horse-traction, because there were no cross-ties, and the clear space between the stone blocks seen in Plate 10 was ideal as a horse track. After the line was first opened there was only one coach a day in each direction. This left Stockton at 7.30 a.m. on Monday, Wednesday, Thursday and Friday; at 3 p.m. on Tuesdays and at 1 p.m. on Saturdays, with the appropriate return services.

As the traffic developed and more coaches were put on, the standard of accommodation for the third-class passengers became increasingly meagre. There does not seem to have been any attempt at running 'mixed' trains—that is trains conveying both passengers and goods. Thus, the expedient adopted on the ceremonial opening day of putting passengers in with the coals was not necessary! But third-class passengers had to stand in open trucks, or ride in the incredibly depressing closed-in boxes illustrated in Plate 23. The horse-drawn coaches had a relatively long innings on the Stockton and Darlington Railway. This was partly due to the slow initial progress of steam locomotive haulage; but once reliable locomotives began to supersede horses on the principal coal hauls the traffic increased to such an extent that there

was not enough room on the line for the privately-owned, toll-paying coaches, and the passenger service became steam-hauled.

24, 25. Stockton and Darlington Railway: Precautions With Steam, The Red Flag Leads; The *Locomotion*, 1825.

When the Stockton and Darlington Railway was opened for public service on 27 September, 1825 the company had only one steam locomotive. This was generally of George Stephenson's 'Killingworth' type, but had a number of improved features to be mentioned later. It was natural that the one and only locomotive should figure prominently in the opening ceremonies. There was nevertheless no small concern at having so relatively novel a machine amid a great concourse of people, who were expected to throng the line-side. Accordingly a number of precautions were taken including a man riding a horse and carrying a red flag a discreet distance ahead of the locomotive! This memorable precaution is shown in Plate 24. Even before the train had got under way the locomotive had given some of the spectators a fright of their lives. Stephenson was getting up steam, and the safety-valve suddenly lifted letting a rush of high-pressure steam escape with a tremendous hiss. Thinking that some fearful explosion was about to take place men, women and children ran for their lives. The train, preceded by the man on horseback, and hauled by the *Locomotion* consisted of no less than 33 wagons, and the 'Experiment' coach, which was reserved for the V.I.P.s.

The *Locomotion* itself (Plate 25), engine No. 1 of the Stockton and Darlington Railway, differed from Stephenson's previous 'Killingworth' engines not only in having greater power, but in two important features of design. In the earlier examples, one cylinder had driven one pair of wheels, and the second the other, while synchronization was maintained by having the two axles connected by a chain passing over two sprocket wheels. In the *Locomotion* Stephenson achieved the same result much more simply by fitting outside crank-pins on the wheels, and coupling the two with a single rod. The 'coupled' engine was universal in later railway days, but *Locomotion* was the first to be so equipped. The other feature of this engine was the design of the wheels. Earlier designs had relatively small wheels made up of forged components, and our picture shows the engine as originally built by Stephenson. The wheels of *Locomotion* were however considerably larger, and at a later time Timothy Hackworth fitted his own type of wheels which were made of a series of cast members carefully fitted together, and surrounded by a single wrought-iron tyre. Wheels of this kind became a familiar feature of Stockton and Darlington locomotives for many years after it was first opened to the public. The *Locomotion* was found capable of hauling a load of 90 tons at speeds of between 6 and 8 m.p.h.

26–28 **Brunel's Broad-Gauge Permanent Way.**

Before proceeding to consider further developments in the early history of the locomotive reference must be made to the very important subject of track. George Stephenson, followed by his son Robert and his brilliant pupil Joseph Locke, adhered in early days to the form of track that had been gradually evolved on the colliery lines of Northumberland and Durham, and embodied in the Stockton

and Darlington Railway. It was from those early lines that the oddest of all standard railway dimensions, the rail gauge, was derived. It was through this early development that a high proportion of the world's railway mileage is laid to a gauge of 4 ft. $8\frac{1}{2}$ in. Today railways throughout western Europe (except Spain), much of Australia and practically the whole of the U.SA. and Canada are laid to this gauge. These countries followed Stephenson's example, and he used it simply because it was the gauge of the Killingworth colliery wagonway! There have been departures from this standard in many countries, but none more defiant than that of I. K. Brunel, Engineer-in-Chief of the Great Western Railway. Brunel considered that 4 ft. $8\frac{1}{2}$ in. was quite inadequate, and recommended 7 ft. The Great Western Board, not without some dissentions, accepted his advice, and the picturesque era of the Broad Gauge was the result.

But Brunel was not content only with having a much wider gauge. He designed an entirely new form of permanent way that differed in almost every conceivable respect from what Stephenson was doing in the north. There was, first of all, the rail itself (Plate 26). This was termed a 'bridge' rail, and it was designed to lie on a continuous longitudinal timber as the old plateways had done. Brunel staked everything upon rigidity of track, and the manner in which he supported the longitudinal timbers emphasized this precept. A cross-section of the permanent way is shown under Plate 28, and it will be seen that he connected the two lines of rails by a common cross-tie thereby intending, no doubt, that one track would give additional rigidity to the other. But the most remarkable, and least successful provision that he made was to support the entire surface framework of timber upon piles driven deep into the ground (Plate 28). It is true that in building the Great Western Railway out of London and following the line of the Thames Valley he was dealing with a very different subsoil to that which Stephenson had encountered in the rough upland country of the northern shires, where the native rock was never far below ground level. No doubt Brunel felt that something more was needed to support the track in the Thames Valley. He certainly built a very splendid and rigid permanent way.

But it was too rigid. Railways had not been in existence for long before it was realized that some springiness in the track was desirable to give a comfortable ride and to ensure that the suspension springs on locomotives and carriages were not shattered by the excessive vibration. There was a case where one of the early railway engineers, having built a line through a rock cutting, fixed the rails directly to the solid rock; but the vibration was so severe that springs, axles, and even wheels were broken daily. Brunel soon found he had to get rid of those piles. After wet weather the ground would subside a little and have the rails hanging in mid-air. But the longitudinal timbers and bridge rails remained to the very end of the broad-gauge era. When lengths of track were relaid with the transverse sleepers standardized everywhere else in Great Britain, the Great Western drivers were quick to notice how much easier their locomotives ran on a track that had some 'spring' in it, and that greater loads could be hauled up a gradient than on a stiff Brunel type of track.

It is curious however that the lessons of history are apt to be overlooked by succeeding generations, and there was a remarkable case of this in 1900 when the deep-level Central London 'tube' railway was opened. This was originally laid with bridge-type rails on continuous longitudinal timbers resting directly on cement in the circle of the tube channel. It was an absolutely rigid track, and things were made worse by the design of the first electric locomotives. The vibration set up was so bad that although the 'tube' was some 70 feet below ground level there was a serious disturbance of many buildings on each side of the line of railway, and the locomotives had to be scrapped. In due course the whole line was relaid with rails resting on conventional supports.

29–30 Two Standard Forms of Track: Bull-Head and Flat-Bottomed or Vignoles Type.

Following upon the discussion of Brunel's novel form of permanent way, as used on the Great Western the early developments towards two standard forms of track may now be mentioned. Although Stephenson, in conjunction with his friend W. Losh, had patented the successful form of rail joint illustrated in Plate 9, he had been ready enough to abandon this when something better was made available. And that 'something better' was the successful rolling at the Bedlington Iron Works, Northumberland, of rails in much longer lengths than it had previously been possible to produce by casting. The use of wrought-iron rails greatly reduced the number of rail joints in the track; but in using the new form of rail Stephenson retained the 'chair' as support, because this provided the most satisfactory method of resting a rail on the big stone blocks that he still considered the ideal track foundation. It was Stephenson's pupil and assistant Joseph Locke who had the idea of so shaping the rails that they were of the same profile top and bottom. It was argued that when they were worn they could be turned over and the previous bottom face made the running surface. But in practice it was found that after a period in service the passage of traffic caused dents and abrasions where a rail had rested in the supporting chairs, and the rail was not fit to be used in the very way intended. But the double-headed rail was developed into the section shown in Plate 29, and became the standard form of track on all British railways, with the rail resting in a substantial cast-iron chair, and wedged tight in position by an oaken key.

At roughly the same time as Locke was developing the Stephenson type of rail another engineer, Charles Blacker Vignoles, who for most of his working life was a strong rival of the Stephenson 'school', was developing the flat-footed end of the Jessop rail (Plate 4) in conjunction with the technique of rolling rails in longer lengths, in wrought iron. The rolling process did not permit of any variation in section, as seen in the cast Jessop rail, but Vignoles designed a flat-bottomed section that should be strong enough to form the 'bridge' between one support and the next, and spiked the rail directly to the timber cross-ties. While not adopted to any extent in Great Britain this form of rail and support became extremely popular, if not entirely universal, abroad. As shown in Plate 30, it was ideal for railways striking out into undeveloped or mountainous countries, where felled trees could be used as cross-ties. It was not necessary to do more than plane a small section to provide a flat surface for the rail to rest upon; otherwise the round section of the tree-trunks could be used just as they were felled. In later years refinements came in

the design and detail of flat-bottomed track; but just as Locke's rail was developed into the standard for the substantially laid tracks at home, so countless overseas railways were, unconsciously perhaps, indebted for their very simple track, to the work of C. B. Vignoles.

31 Timothy Hackworth's *Royal George*, 1827.

Following the successful opening of the Stockton and Darlington Railway, George Stephenson's services were much in demand as a consultant in connection with many railway projects. He had many staunch friends among the directors and top management of the railway, and they were pleased and proud to know that their engineer was in such demand, and raised no objection to his absences in other parts of the country. At the same time the position of the resident locomotive engineer was no sinecure. Timothy Hackworth had this job. He had been foreman at Stephenson's works at Newcastle, and had the job of running the Killingworth type of locomotives on the Stockton and Darlington Railway. In continuous service they gave much trouble, and were frequently deficient in steaming capacity. Hackworth made history by reconstructing a six-coupled engine that had been obtained from Wilson's of Leeds. This was the celebrated *Royal George*; it was not only one of the very first locomotives to have *six* wheels coupled, but it had a greatly improved boiler. This latter had a return flue, like Hedley's *Puffing Billy*, but it also incorporated one of the first examples of a 'blast-pipe' in the chimney, designed to sharpen the draught on the fire, and improve the steaming. The engine drew loads of 100 tons at 5 m.p.h. on level track.

Our picture shows Hackworth's type of wheel, which was fitted in due course to the *Locomotion*.

32 **Rainhill Competitors 1:** Robert Stephenson's *Rocket*.

When George Stephenson was appointed engineer to the Liverpool and Manchester Railway one can be sure that he had no thoughts other than it would be a steam-operated railway. But the troubles with locomotives on the Stockton and Darlington, with which Timothy Hackworth was having to cope, were not lost upon a section of the Liverpool and Manchester Board, which had opposed the appointment of Stephenson, and which favoured horse or cable traction. In due course however the Directors offered a prize of £500 for the best locomotive to work the line. Very complete details were laid down as to the performance required, and to avoid any kind of confusion each locomotive was tested on a separate day. The *Rocket*, built by Robert Stephenson, was the only one of the four steam locomotives entered to complete the course of ten return trips in rapid succession over a length of $1\frac{1}{2}$ miles. The test length was actually $1\frac{3}{4}$ miles, but one-eighth of a mile at each end was allowed for stopping and restarting. The *Rocket* was a simple and straightforward engine, and performed consistently well, hauling a load of $12\frac{3}{4}$ tons at an average speed of 15 m.p.h. When really opened out a speed of 24 m.p.h. was attained. The engine itself weighed $4\frac{1}{2}$ tons.

33 **Rainhill Competitors 2:** Timothy Hackworth's *Sanspareil*.

It was typical of the dogged perseverance of Timothy Hackworth that he should have been emboldened to enter a loco-

motive of his own design and construction in the Rainhill trials against that of the son of his former chief. But Hackworth felt that in his boiler, as fitted to the *Royal George*, he had a definite advantage over anything the Stephenson's had so far produced. He designed the engine in his spare time, and although the Stockton and Darlington Railway allowed him to build the engine in the Company's works at Shildon, it was done at his own expense. Unlike the *Rocket*, which had but a single pair of driving wheels, the *Sanspareil* was four-coupled. It was slightly overweight for a four-wheeled engine, and had it managed to stay the course some difficulty might have arisen in judging its performance. Actually, however, after making some good runs with a load of 19 tons, the feed-pump supplying water to the boiler failed and the trials had to be stopped. Hackworth's learned biographer, Robert Young, has stated that one of the cylinders burst, although no report of any such occurrence appears in the official account of the trials. But the feed-pump failure was in itself enough to put the *Sanspareil* out of the running.

34 **Rainhill Competitors 3:** Ericsson and Braithwaite's *Novelty*.

This strange-looking machine, which fully justified its name, was designed jointly by Ericsson and Braithwaite, and was from the very start of the competition the popular favourite. It was beautifully finished, and compared very favourably with the *Rocket* in this respect. The latter was a plain, workmanlike job, whereas there was a rare touch of showmanship about the *Novelty* that naturally appealed to the spectators. It had a vertical boiler, and the necessary draught for rapid steam raising was provided by a set of mechanically-worked bellows. There was only one cylinder, fixed almost vertically above the rear pair of wheels. It proved a very swift runner, and thrilled the crowd by dashing past the grandstand at 23 m.p.h. on a preliminary run, but she never completed a single series of trials. The bellows kept going wrong, and despite some very spectacular sprints, the *Novelty* had to be disqualified. It was a great pity that purely mechanical faults dogged the running of a locomotive of such possibilities. On one occasion a speed of 40 m.p.h. was attained. But in the event the *Rocket* was left as the winner, and as the only engine competing that fulfilled the conditions and finished the entire series of trials without mishap.

35 Liverpool and Manchester Railway: The Moorish Arch.

The first public railway in the world, the Stockton and Darlington, was built strictly upon utilitarian lines. It was not in George Stephenson's hard-headed, north-country outlook to suggest anything in the way of adornments, either for the equipment or the buildings; but it was another matter when the railway network began to extend and businessmen with an eye to publicity were elected to the railway boards. The Liverpool and Manchester line climbed out of the Liverpool terminus on a steep gradient that was at first operated by cable haulage, but when level track was reached at what is now Edge Hill, and the deep, vertical-sided Olive Mount cutting lay ahead, the tracks were spanned by a magnificent ornamental archway in the Moorish style. The designer's name is not generally known, but it would certainly not have been George Stephenson. As engineer he had to build it, and it formed the centre-piece of the inaugural ceremonies when the line was officially opened by the Duke of Wellington. It was on that occasion, too, that the tragic accident occurred to William Huskisson, who, not looking before he alighted from a carriage, descended right in the path of an oncoming train and was fatally injured. The Moorish Arch, sybolical though it was, did not last for long for the very practical reason that increasing traffic demanded a wider line, and the arch had to be taken down.

36 Liverpool and Manchester Railway: A Wayside Station.

The wayside stations on this line were all neatly designed, and immaculately kept. The Liverpool and Manchester immediately after its inception took on a character that was quite different from that of the Stockton and Darlington. The latter was essentially a mineral carrier. Passengers were quite a secondary consideration. But while the proprietors of the Liverpool and Manchester Railway hoped to attract a great deal of freight traffic, particularly from the Bridgwater Canal, it immediately became a major passenger line. As will be shown later in this book excellent provision was made for all three classes of passengers, and passengers were for some time its principal source of revenue. The trains made many stops, and arrangements were provided at the stations for replenishing the water tanks of the locomotives. There were no platforms at the lineside, and passengers walked about as they pleased. Although the death of Mr. Huskisson at the opening ceremony undoubtedly sounded a warning to people not to wander across the tracks, at first nothing appears to have been done to fence in the right of way! Contemporary pictures suggest that earth covering was piled over the stone blocks of the permanent way up to a level little below that of the running edge of the rails.

37 London and Birmingham Railway: The Doric Arch, Euston.

Important and successful as the Liverpool and Manchester Railway was, it did not represent a 'main line' in the modern sense of the word, and one of the earliest of these latter was the London and Birmingham, a line 112 miles long. In more than one sense however this line was a veritable gateway to the North from London, and for twelve years it was the only northbound railway exit from the Capital. The entrance to the station, in what was then known as Euston Grove, was adorned with the stupendous Doric Arch, completed in 1838. Its size and magnificent appearance was certainly appropriate to the significance of the London and Birmingham Railway, and although it afterwards became encompassed with many other buildings, and its grand vista obscured, it remained a feature of Euston station for 120 years. The railway itself became first the London and North Western, then the London, Midland and Scottish, and finally the London Midland Region of the nationalized British Railways. It was not only lovers of the historic, and picturesque who were disappointed that this great archway, designed by Philip Hardwick, could not have been incorporated in the redesign of the station that was necessary when the line was electrified; but those responsible said no, and the Arch was demolished in 1962.

38 London and Birmingham Railway: Curzon Street Station, Birmingham.

The geographical situation of the City of Birmingham is peculiar and perhaps almost unique in that it does not occupy a natural site beside a river, nor is it at an ancient point of highway junctions, but instead is perched on the top of a hill. When Robert Stephenson laid out the course of the London and Birmingham Railway, he fixed the site of the northern terminus at the foot of the hill. There was enough trouble at the London end, with the very steep gradient leading from Camden Town down into Euston, and he obviously did not want to be troubled with gradients by taking the railway up the hill into the heart of Birmingham. But whatever the location, the station had to have an impressive façade, and the entrance, although not so exquisitely grand as the Doric Arch at Euston, was splendid all the same, and again in the classical style. When the railway was continued north from Birmingham, by the building of the Grand Junction line, Curzon Street became the departure point for the north as well as for the south, with the Grand Junction Railway taking a leftwards wheel shortly after leaving the terminus. Later developments demanded a central city station in Birmingham, and Curzon Street then became the goods station of the London and North Western Railway. So it has remained, under successive changes in ownership, and whereas the Doric Arch has been demolished, the classical façade of Curzon Street remains today, grimy yet still impressive among all the hurly-burly of freight business.

39–40 Liverpool and Manchester Railway: Passenger Rolling-Stock.

Reference has already been made to the importance placed upon passenger traffic by the management of this immediately most successful railway. Accommodation was provided for first-, second- and third-class passengers, though the three classes were not generally conveyed in the same train—in the earliest days at any rate. In broad terms the first-class carriages were entirely closed in; the seconds were open at the sides, but with a canopy to provide some protection from the weather and from the sparks and smuts emitted by the locomotives; and the third-class carriages were just plain trucks, entirely open, with plank seats inside. On second- and third-class trains there appears to have been no special provision for luggage. Passengers of those orders were not expected to take much with them, and nothing that could not be lifted into the ordinary carriages. It might be taken as a figment of the artist's imagination to have many individuals in tall hats sitting in open 'thirds'; but our pictures have been prepared from contemporary drawings by such masters as Bourne and Talbot Bury, and at that period in history the tall hat was the standard form of male headgear, for rich and poor alike.

The sight of trim young ladies in poke bonnets might raise thoughts as to what those bonnets and their cloaks would be like at the *end* of a journey in one of those third-class carriages; but in those pioneer days, and particularly on the Liverpool and Manchester, the emission of smoke of any kind was regarded as a case of gross mismanagement on the part of the enginemen, and in this respect they were assisted by the almost universal use of coke as a fuel, rather than raw coal. The improvements in locomotive design that enabled coal to be used without creating too much smoke came much later. The first-class coaches were built in the style of the old stage-coaches, and Plate 39 shows one of these adapted for carrying mails. On all these early first-

class railway coaches there was one important difference from road vehicles, in that there were no outside passengers. The only person travelling outside was the guard. First-class carriages had provision for carrying luggage on the roofs, and many are the tales told of the inconvenience experienced by passengers at intermediate stations from men climbing on to roofs to load or unload. Furthermore, there was always the danger of sparks from the locomotive lodging among the various packages and causing fires. No calamity is on record as arising from this hazard, and by the time coal was superseding coke as a locomotive fuel separate luggage vans, or compartments were being provided on the trains.

41–42 Liverpool and Manchester Railway: Conveyance of Livestock.

The establishment of public railways introduced the principle of the 'common carrier'. They were required by law to carry any traffic that was offered. The Stockton and Darlington, which was enterprised primarily as a glorified colliery line, experienced the 'common carrier' business to no more than a limited extent in its early days, and then largely on its own initiative in seeking return loads to convey in the trains of empty coal wagons returning from Stockton to the Bishop Auckland district. But it was not long before the Liverpool and Manchester Railway, in modern slang, 'had the lot'. Interspersed with their profitable passenger business they were called upon to carry all kinds of merchandise from the Liverpool docks to Machester, and a simple all-purpose freight four-wheeler like the Stockton and Darlington colliery cauldron was out of the question. Commodious open wagons were piled high with all sorts of loads, carefully sheeted to protect the content from the weather and the emissions of the locomotives.

Then there was the question of livestock. From time immemorial the Englishman has been kind to animals. He thinks nothing of packing his fellow men and women into carriages like sardines, and some present-day commuter trains in the London area could give the Liverpool and Manchester 'thirds' points and a beating for the number of persons to the square yard! But animals—no! And from the very inception of the Liverpool and Manchester Railway, its responsibilities in the conveyance of livestock were taken most seriously. Plates 41 and 42 show two types of special vehicle operating on the line in the early 1830s. With some of the larger breeds of animal, such as pigs and cattle arrangements were made for the drovers to travel with them, to be on hand if any of these 'passengers' became restive or unruly. After all it must be remembered that these early livestock wagons were very light both in construction and in dead weight, and half a dozen rampaging cows could probably overturn the vehicles. The traditional docility of sheep, once they were herded into their cages, permitted more economical methods of conveyance. Without any overcrowding, they could be contained in double-decked vans, and in this respect the Liverpool and Manchester Railway provided the prototype for many huge, double-decked bogie sheep wagons in service today on a number of overseas railways.

43 Mohawk and Hudson Railroad: The *De Witt Clinton*, 1831.

Up to the present, the illustrations and references in this book have been entirely British, as is appropriate in view of the nigh thirty years of pioneer development during the first decade of the nineteenth century. But even before the Liverpool and Manchester Railway was opened, the first railways were working in the U.S.A. in 1827, and in France in 1828, and it is now time to look at some of these developments. The *De Witt Clinton* was the first locomotive to run in New York State, and was built by the West Point Foundry Association for the Mohawk and Hudson Railroad Company, in 1831. This curious little engine had the cylinders at the rear, mounted inclined on either side of the footplate and driving on to the leading pair of coupled wheels. These latter were 4 ft. 6 in. diameter and gave the engine a good turn of speed. When pulling a load of 8 tons, a maximum of 30 m.p.h. was attained. The engine itself does not appear to have been very satisfactory, and it was scrapped in 1835. The pieces realized about $485. But as the first locomotive of what became the New York Central Railroad its memory has become venerated. A full-sized operable replica was built by the New York Central and Hudson River Railroad, as the system was then known in its own shops at West Albany (N.Y.) in 1893 for exhibition at the World's Columbian Exposition in Chicago, and it has subsequently been shown in many exhibitions. In between these occasions it was regularly on display on a balcony inside the Grand Central Terminal Station in New York, but since 1935 it has been on loan to the Henry Ford Museum at Dearborn.

44 Mohawk and Hudson Railroad: A First-Class Carriage.

The various appearances of the replica *De Witt Clinton* locomotive were usually accompanied by a train of three carriages of contemporary build, constructed as replicas, to be hauled by the locomotive. It is extremely interesting to compare this carriage with the early British 'first', as running on the Liverpool and Manchester Railway at about the same time. In the first place the American coach is designed for both inside and outside passengers. The base frame is extended front and rear, and the flap gives access to the central step by which outside passengers climbed up to sit three abreast at each end of the roof. The padded 'back' to the seat will be seen from our picture, while the cross platform just above the centre step provided a foot-rest. There were seats at each end of the roof so that a full complement of 'outside' passengers would consist of three facing the engine at the forward, and three back to the engine at the rear. The space between the two seat-backs was available for luggage. On exhibition runs it seemed that the outside seats were more popular than the inside, and usually taken by young ladies in white dresses and 'picture' hats. How they fared from smuts and sparks is not recorded, for in her 'replica' condition the *De Witt Clinton* was, more often than not, fired with wood blocks.

45 Baltimore and Ohio Railroad: The Imlay Carriage.

This was the first railway to be constructed in the U.S.A. and British enthusiasts will recall that it was for the centenary celebrations in 1927 that the Great Western locomotive, *King George V*, was shipped across the Atlantic. The early locomotives were of a curious appearance, with vertical boilers known in the U.S.A. as 'Grasshoppers', but our picture shows the remarkable development of the double-deck type of carriage. The bodies, like those of the Mohawk and Hudson Railroad were gondola-shaped, but in addition to seating three facing and three back to the engine front and rear there was seating for a dozen or more persons on the top on a double-sided, bench-type seat. The curtains and canopies will be noted, particularly those beneath the seats. The interior had side curtains that could be lowered if necessary. The method of suspending this elaborate and ornate body from the basic frame suggests that much thought had been given to the problem of giving a comfortable ride, though one would imagine that there was then little thought of speed; otherwise those curtains, hanging loose, would have been no end of a nuisance. Passengers in crinolines riding on the upper deck might also have found any speed embarrassing! There were many forms of colour finish. Some were garishly adorned with large lettering, and figures representing the insignia of speed.

46 Camden and Amboy Railroad: An Early Bogie Coach.

This line, which became part of the giant Pennsylvania system, began operations in 1831, with what is now the oldest complete and operable steam locomotive in the U.S.A. This is an 0–4–0 built by Robert Stephenson & Co. of Newcastle-on-Tyne, and was virtually of the improved Liverpool and Manchester 'goods' type. For service in the U.S.A. it had to have a cowcatcher, and this was supported by a two-wheeled pony truck, or 'pilot', which was added in 1832. But the main purpose of the pilot truck was to guide the locomotive on the sharp curves built into the line. It was for this same purpose that at a very early date the American railways began to depart from the traditional British four-wheeled chassis for both passenger and freight cars. For easy running on sharply curved tracks, the Americans began to develop the long car running on two four-wheeled bogies. This not only provided a degree of flexibility but gave better running on roughly-laid tracks. Reference has already been made to the ready adoption of the Vignoles flat-bottomed rail, spiked directly to the cross-ties; the short wheel-based bogies on American eight-wheeled cars adapted themselves easily to any inequalities or irregularities in the road, and in due course it became the standard type of vehicle for both passenger and freight traffic. Our picture shows a very early example used on the Camden and Amboy Railroad in the early 1830s.

47 St. Etienne and Andrezieux Railway: Passenger Train Haulage.

This first railway in France, opened in 1828, was not a public one. It was built primarily for the conveyance of coal, and like the early English colliery lines relied to a great extent upon horse traction. But the line eventually became part of the great Paris, Lyons and Mediterranean system and in the archives of that company there was a series of paintings depicting early days on the St. Etienne line. These show a variation of passenger rolling-stock, mostly drawn by horses. Our picture shows what might be imagined to be a double-headed coach; but actually it seems that two horses in tandem were used to haul anything up to four coaches. A typical train would consist of two of the closed-in type as shown in Plate 47 and two of the double-deckers, Plate 48. The old pictures previously referred to indicate

that although the coaches were coupled in trains, each had its own coachman, riding in the front, as shown in Plate 47. Two horses in tandem had to pull as many as seven wagons loaded with a variety of merchandise, though there is evidence to show that at least some of the trains were hauled by steam locomotives of a very primitive type. These look as if they were of the 'return flue' type like the English *Puffing Billy*, because the fireman is shown riding on an out-rigged platform in front of the chimney.

48 St. Etienne and Andrezieux Railway: Double-Decker Passenger Coach.

The early paintings in the archives of the former P.L.M. Railway show several types of double-decker coach, arranged in the form of one of the old-fashioned trams, with open top decks, so familiar in English towns sixty or seventy years ago. The lower deck had handsome side curtains, but the early drawings do not make it clear how people managed to climb to the upper deck. None of the fascinating contemporary pictures show anything in the way of a ladder! There is reason to believe that the St. Etienne line indulged in a fair amount of gravity working on inclines, after the English North Country style. Not only this, but the pictures suggest that gravity working was also used for passenger coaches. In Plate 48 the coachman is on his own, supposedly controlling the speed on an incline by application of some form of brake. There is indeed an old painting in existence that shows a train of six passenger coaches gliding downhill under the influence of gravity. It consists of three closed-in, first-class carriages at the front, and then three double-checkers, each with its 'coachman' sitting on the front. While there is no precise evidence to indicate that the St. Etienne line was ever worked in this way, the references are most interesting, as showing the general attitude to railways in the late 1820s. Horses and gravity were then more in fashion than locomotives!

49 Brussels and Malines Railways: Passenger Coach.

Until the year 1835 only France and the U.S.A. had followed Great Britain in the construction of railways, and the only French line in existence was the private St. Etienne, the rolling-stock of which has just been described. But in 1835 public railways were opened in both Belgium and Germany, and the first public railways in France followed in 1837. In Belgium the pioneer line, the Brussels and Malines was like its predecessors in England and the U.S.A. a private company, authorised by law to render public transport, and for many years the Belgian Government continued to grant concessions for the construction of railways by private companies. A great number of small lines—many competing with one another—grew up; but in 1870 the Government decided to end the policy of granting private concessions. All existing lines were taken over by the State, and general co-ordination of facilities commenced. The 'coach', for open passengers on the Brussels and Malines Railway is no more than typical of the way humble folks were glad enough to travel in the early days of railways.

50 Stockton and Darlington Railway: Closed-in Passenger Coach.

Under Plates 22 and 23, mention was made of the practice on this railway of licensing private hauliers to run horse-drawn coaches for passengers on payment of appropriate tolls. Some of these coaches, constructed on the most frugal and parsimonious lines, were forbidding in their stark austerity, and except in the most severe of winter weather, one feels it would have been preferable to ride 'open' as depicted in the Brussels and Malines wagon rather than suffer from claustrophobia in the glorified 'dog-kennel' on wheels shown in Plate 50. The evolution of railway carriages for the lower orders of travellers came most reluctantly in all countries, and the story of how some of the less-enlightened English companies met the legislation that was imposed upon them in 1844 now making amusing reading, in the later sections of this book.

51–53 The Atmospheric System of Propulsion.

Steam railways had not been in existence for long before inventors were seeking 'improved' methods of traction, and one of these was the 'Atmospheric'. In its broadest sense this was akin to modern electric traction, as it avoided the use of self-contained power unit on the train. In the Atmospheric system, a large pipe was laid down the middle of the track as shown in Plates 52 and 53, and the air was exhausted from this pipe by a series of pumping engine houses along the line. The trains had no locomotives as such, but instead a traction carriage, as shown in Plate 51. This carriage had suspended from it a carrying gear which was connected to a piston fitting snugly into the pipe that ran the length of the track. The air was exhausted from the pipe ahead of the piston, and the suction thus created hauled the train along.

It will be appreciated however that the piston, in the tube, had somehow to be connected with the traction carriage gear and this proved the underlying weakness in the system. The cross-sectional picture, Plate 52, shows how the pipe was sealed, when there was no train about, by a leather flap, shown in red. The traction carriage had an attachment that pushed this flap up to the angle shown just for the moment when the carriage was passing so that the pipe was normally sealed throughout its length and just opened sufficiently to let the suspending gear of the traction carriage pass along. It was first tried out on a line near Dublin, and worked sufficiently well to attract the attention of I. K. Brunel, the Engineer-in-Chief of the Great Western Railway and its associated broad-gauge lines in the West of England. It appealed to him immensely, not only in its avoidance of the smoke, dirt and labour of operating steam locomotives, but because the central power plant, as represented by the pumping machinery in the stationary engine houses gave promise of greater power for hauling the trains.

He recommended its use for the South Devon Railway, planned to run between Exeter and Plymouth, and confident in the high tractive power that would be available he took the line through the very hilly country on the southern flanks of Dartmoor on some exceedingly steep gradients to lessen the initial cost of construction. When first put into commission on the level stretch of line from Exeter round the coastal section to Newton Abbot, the 'Atmospheric' worked well, and the trains were taken with a quietness and absence of effort that delighted the passengers. But then the rats and the sea air began to affect the leather flap; and as the efficacy of that flap was the very cornerstone of the whole system, troubles began to develop. The flap no longer sealed the tube. The pumping machine could not

overcome the leakage from the top of the tube, and the suction available to haul the trains dwindled to nothing. Trains were left stranded in the open country. There was nothing their crews could do. Of course the leather was renewed, but again it lasted no time, and after some desperate struggles to keep things going, Brunel had to admit failure and convert the line to ordinary locomotive haulage. The 'Atmospheric' lasted barely three years, and in the end all that was left to be seen of this courageous experiment were the picturesque pumping stations (Plate 53) with their campanile towers, and the exceedingly steep gradients west of Newton Abbot.

54 South Carolina Canal and Railroad Co.: The *Best Friend of Charleston*, 1830.

This extraordinary looking machine was built in 1830 by the West Point Foundry Association. So far as its machinery was concerned, it was a simple and straightforward 0-4-0, but its remarkable feature was the boiler. This, as will be seen from our picture, was vertical in the form of an old-fashioned porter-bottle. The firebox was at the bottom surrounded by water, and the inside was full of what were called teats, running out from the sides and top, with alternate stays to support the crown of the firebox. It was the first steam locomotive in America to operate on a regularly scheduled run. Its cost is given at $4000, which at the rate of exchange then prevailing would be a little less than £1000. It was despatched by sea from New York to Charleston, and made its first public run on Christmas Day 1830. The line then extended for no more than six miles out of Charleston; but it was rapidly extended and by October 1833 the full 136 miles to

Hamburg had been completed, making it the longest continuous length of railway anywhere in the world at that time. Some two years before then, however, the career of the *Best Friend of Charleston* came to a sudden and violent end. One of those riding on her, in an attempt to get more power, held the safety-valve closed, with the result that the boiler burst; and that was the end of what appears to have been a very satisfactory locomotive.

55 West Point Foundry: The *Experiment*, 1832 (later named *Brother Jonathon*).

During the first five years of pioneer railroading in the U.S.A., locomotives had either been imported from England or built to some extent on the English model. They were all four-wheelers, like the *Stourbridge Lion*, built by Foster, Eastrick & Co. of Stourbridge, and the *America*, which was built by Robert Stephenson & Co, in 1828. They were entirely in the English tradition, and either of the two mentioned would have passed for a standard locomotive on the Stockton and Darlington, or the Liverpool and Manchester Railways. The *De Witt Clinton*, and the *Best Friend of Charleston*, although looking so different, had the same kind of chassis arrangement and all were alike in taking unkindly to to American track. It was in face of these circumstances that the *Experiment* was built in 1832 at West Point Foundry. It was a new conception, designed by John B. Jervis, specially to suit American track. Instead of having all wheels mounted in a fixed frame, only the single pair of rear drivers was carried directly on the frame. The fore part of the locomotive was supported on a swivel truck which readily adjusted itself to the curves and inequalities of the track, and provided an easy and safe

riding locomotive. This proposition was the invention of M. W. Baldwin, founder of the world-famous Baldwin Locomotive Company. The *Experiment* was so successful that Baldwin's built well over 100 locomotives of the 4–2–0 type between 1834 and 1842.

56 Baltimore and Ohio Railroad: The *Lafayette*, 1837, a Norris 'One-Armed Billy'.

The success of the *Experiment*, so far as its good tracking qualities were concerned, led to American builders other than Baldwin developing the 4–2–0 type. The products of William Norris, of Philadelphia, became deservedly famous and the *Lafayette*, shown in our picture was at one and the same time the first locomotive on the Baltimore and Ohio Railroad to have a horizontal boiler, and the first to have more than four wheels. Norris used the short wheel-based bogie used by Baldwin. A notable feature of this early Norris engine was the use of the hay-stack type of firebox, characteristic of the early broad-gauge locomotives on the Great Western Railway in England. The *Lafayette* was considered of such historical significance, that a full-sized operable replica was built by the Baltimore and Ohio Railroad in 1927 to run during the centenary celebrations of that company in that year. The Norris 4–2–0s had a useful design feature in having the driving axle ahead of the firebox. This made possible a more advantageous distribution of the weight, and greater adhesion on the driving axle. It is not without significance that some engines of this type were imported into England for use on the Lickey Incline, above all places, where the gradient is 1 in 37 for two miles.

57 Stockton and Darlington Railway: The *Wilberforce*, 1831.

While American engineers were finding it necessary to secure increased flexibility of wheelbase to run on their native tracks, no such need seems to have arisen on the parent of all steam railways. Timothy Hackworth, having obtained reliable steaming and good tractive power with the *Royal George* (Plate 31), proceeded to develop the design for general mineral train haulage. The *Wilberforce*, and similar engines of the same design, had vertical cylinders on either side of the driver's footplate and the drive was taken through a dummy crankshaft immediately below, instead of driving direct to a crank-pin on the rearmost driving wheel, as in the *Royal George*. The *Wilberforce* was the prototype for a considerable series of six-coupled mineral train engines on the Stockton and Darlington Railway. As improved methods of suspension were developed Hackworth abandoned his vertical cylinders and drove directly on to the wheels. The need for having the firedoor on the chimney end of the boiler has already been mentioned. Our picture of the *Wilberforce* shows the entire outfit, with the small tender containing the coal, and space for the fireman ahead of the engine, and a second tender, carrying the large barrelled water tank at the opposite end.

58 The Admiralty Semaphores.

Good communication is a fundamental necessity of any transport system, and when railways were in their infancy it must be remembered that such inventions as the electric telegraph had not been made. The means of long-distance message convey-ance devised in times of national emergency may be recalled. First, at the time of the Spanish Armada in 1588, warning that the Armada had been sighted was conveyed across the length and breadth of England by a chain of huge bonfires kindled on hill-tops from which they could be seen many miles away. When the threat of a Napoleonic invasion existed, a series of semaphore signal-posts was set up between Portsmouth and London, and our picture shows how these were positioned so that the indication of one could be transmitted to the next one. What the actual indications signified is not known; but this form of signal formed the basis of what eventually proved to be the standard form of mechanical signalling on the British railways. Contemporary drawings from which our picture has been prepared, do not however indicate how messages would be conveyed at night.

59–61 Primitive Forms of Railway Warning Signals.

When pioneer railway operations had reached the point where it was necessary to give some indication to the driver, the overriding consideration was to tell him when and where to stop. Red was the natural colour to signify danger, and our pictures show three simple forms of saying 'Stop'. The examples, Plates 59 and 60, are similar in that the target, or flag, was mounted on a vertical shaft that could be rotated. The handle sticking out at the bottom of the mast enabled the shaft to be turned so that the red board was edge-on to the driver and thus practically invisible. In this latter position it could be assumed that the danger was removed and that the train could proceed. The 'ball' signal worked in the same way. It was hauled up to the top of the post to indicate danger, and lowered to ground level when it was safe to proceed. The weakness with all three types was that if by any chance the board, or target, became broken off, or the chain holding the ball aloft broke no indication would be given, and in the absence of a red warning the driver could assume it was safe to proceed, whereas in actual fact there was danger ahead—all the more serious because the warning of it had failed to be given.

62 **Paris and St. Germain Railway:** First-Class Carriage.

This was one of the first public railways to be opened in France, in 1837. It had a length of thirteen miles, and eventually became one of the suburban routes of the Ouest system. It is interesting to recall that at its first opening, part of this line was worked on the 'Atmospheric' system, thus preceding the adoption of that system by Brunel, for the South Devon Railway, by about seven years. Other parts of the Paris and St. Germain line were operated by steam locomotives. The carriage shown in our picture having sides open except for a grillage, with curtains behind, is interesting because of the contrast it provides to the practice adopted soon afterwards on certain other French lines, of having closed-in carriages and locking the doors before starting. This turned what might have been little more than a minor derailment on the Paris and Versailles Railway into a terrible disaster. The leading engine of a double-headed train broke its front axle, and went down 'on its nose', so to speak. The second engine crashed on top of it, and many of the lightly constructed wooden coaches followed. But the doors were locked, and the unfortunate passengers could not get

out before the whole of the leading part of the train took fire. Many were burned to death before axes and other appliances could be brought to break open the locked doors.

63 **Newcastle and South Shields Railway:** Passenger Carriage.

From the earliest days of railway, much care was devoted to the adornment of locomotives on the majority of railways. There were exceptions, of course, like Timothy Hackworth's work-a-day, six-coupleds on the Stockton and Darlington (Plate 57). But after the early days of fanciful first-class carriages, in the style of the old stage-coaches, not a great deal of attention was paid to the outward decoration of carriages—or the inside for that matter, where second- and third-class passengers were concerned. There was little interworking of stock between the different companies, where their lines adjoined, and the principal concern in the outward painting of carriages was to make a clear distinction between the different classes. Many passengers of the lower orders were illiterate, and could not read any inscriptions on the sides, so the coaches were painted in brightly distinctive colours. This example, from a busy local line in Northumberland, that became part of the North Eastern Railway, is typical of the painting styles adopted in certain areas.

64–65 **French Railways:** A Road-Railer Carriage.

One of the most familiar features of early travel on British railways was for the more wealthy patrons to arrange for their own private carriages to be conveyed on flat trucks, and attached at the rear of regular passenger trains. The complete carriage was transported, being run up a ramp, on its own wheels, and then firmly secured in position. The emphasis was laid on 'firm' securing, because tales are told of wealthy passengers (who, for political or other reasons, were unpopular in certain districts) having the fastenings of their coaches loosened, or secured in a deliberately slip-shod fashion to cause the coach to come adrift in transit. But this French example, shown in Plates 64 and 65, is of a different kind altogether. This is a coach body designed to be conveyed either by road or railway. There was a four-wheeled trolley on which the body was mounted for road usage, and then the body was lifted and transferred laterally to a waiting railway vehicle. The coach body was quite a large affair, with three compartments and a remarkable hooded canopy for the driver. There was a special gallery over the area where the transfer from road to rail took place. This was indeed a most astonishing prototype of the modern practice used in connection with the Freightliner service on British Railways. At the terminals the overhead gallery principle is used, though of course today all is done by completely mechanized plant, as compared to the hand winches shown in our pictures. On seeing these pictures, and comparing them with the layout in a modern freightliner terminal, one could indeed remark that 'there is nothing new under the sun'!

66 The First Steam Locomotive in Germany: *Der Adler*.

In 1833, Robert Stephenson had produced a development of the standard 2–2–0 used on the Liverpool and Manchester Railway with a sufficient number of new, if not necessarily novel, features for him to secure a patent on the design. It was little more than an enlargement of the 2–2–0, but of the 2–2–2 wheel arrangement to permit carrying a longer and heavier boiler. It was accepted as probably the best all-round passenger engine of the day, and the first steam locomotive to run in Germany, *Der Adler* of the Nuremberg–Furth Railway, was of this type, built at Stephenson's Newcastle works in 1835. Like all Robert Stephenson's early locomotive designs it was extremely simple, with outside frames throughout, and an enormously tall chimney of very small diameter. Engines of this type, extensively used in England, were also copied by various continental firms. As far as was possible the firm of Robert Stephenson & Co. maintained a fairly close scrutiny over locomotives built to their drawings in foreign lands, so that the essential reliability of the product was maintained. In course of time *Der Adler* has become one of the most famous of historical locomotives, so much so that today it is included in a series of elegant little match-box models.

67 Stockton and Darlington Railway: 2–2–0 Locomotive, *Sunbeam*.

By the year 1837, when this quaint little engine was built, the 2–2–0 type was becoming a good deal less common on the railways of Great Britain. Already there was a demand for larger and more powerful units. But then the Newcastle firm of R. & W. Hawthorn received an order for four of these tiny little things, weighing no more than 9¾ tons, for the New York, Boston and Providence Railway in the U.S.A. Whether or not the Americans thought better of it when they had placed the order cannot be stated for certain, but the fact remains that Hawthorn's were left with three out of the four engines on their hands. Two were eventually sold to the Paris and Versailles Railway, and the remaining one was bought by the Stockton and Darlington. This is the engine, *Sunbeam*, illustrated in our picture. From the machinery point of view, it was an almost exact replica of Stephenson's earlier *Planet* type 2–2–0s on the Liverpool and Manchester Railway. Since the Rainhill trials, a rift had occurred between Timothy Hackworth and the Stephensons, and in his capacity as locomotive superintendent of the Stockton and Darlington railway one can only assume Hackworth was particularly short of engines to agree to purchase one of Stephenson's design, even though it had been built by Hawthorns. Nevertheless, the *Sunbeam* put in many years of good work on the Stockton and Darlington Railway.

68 Liverpool and Manchester Railway: A Bury 0–4–0, the *Liverpool*.

The Liverpool and Manchester Railway had scarcely opened before the Stephensons had rivals in the locomotive-building business. In addition to Hackworth. One of these was Edward Bury, who was the technical driving force of the firm of Bury, Curtis and Kennedy. Bury was strongly endowed with the commercial instinct, and from the very outset he was striving with might and main to undercut Stephenson's prices. The outcome of this was his use of bar, instead of plate frames. This gave his engines a spidery-looking appearance when seen broadside. Our picture shows the famous 0–4–0 *Liverpool* which looks for all the world as if it is no more than a boiler on wheels! Bury's engines were all soundly constructed and many of them had extraordinarily long lives. The

Liverpool, built in 1830, had the largest coupled wheels yet seen on a locomotive, 6 ft. in diameter, and the characteristic 'hay-stack' type of firebox. Another pleasing touch was the series of ornamental Liver birds around the top of the chimney. In 1927, when the new Royal Scot class of 4–6–0 was put into service on the London, Midland and Scottish Railway, and a number were named after historic locomotives, the *Liverpool* was one of those selected for honourable remembrance on the L.M.S.R. engine No. 6130.

69. Dublin and Kingstown Railway: A Forrester 2–2–0, the *Vauxhall*.

Among the many locomotive building firms that sprang up in the 1830s in England, was that of George Forrester, of Liverpool. At that time it seemed that each manufacturer deliberately set out to introduce features different from those of all others. Forrester set out to get the machinery from beneath the boiler. This of course would have been no more than a reversion to the earliest practice, if Forrester had not arranged his cylinders horizontally, and with the cross-head guides formed by a downward extension of the framing. In addition to the Irish engines, of which the *Vauxhall* in our picture is an example, Forrester built engines of this type for the Liverpool and Manchester Railway, and some for the first railway in London, the London and Greenwich. In their original form they were not a success. The wide spacing of the cylinders, at the extreme outside width of the frames, caused excessive swaying when they began to attain any speed, and in consequence they earned the nickname of the 'boxers'. Nevertheless the design is important for the way the arrangement of cylinders and front-end framing was adapted by a master hand, Alexander Allan, to produce one of the most successful and reliable types in the later years of the period covered by this book (*see* Plate 163).

70 **Liverpool and Manchester Railway:** The *Lion*.

This deservedly famous engine is perhaps better known under her 'stage name' of the *Titfield Thunderbolt*, from the exciting part she played in the film of that name in 1953. She was built in 1838 by Tod Kitson and Laird, of Leeds, for the Liverpool and Manchester Railway for goods service, and eventually went into the ownership of the London and North Western. She led a relatively humdrum existence as a goods engine, and in 1859 was sold to the Mersey Docks and Harbour Board. They did not want her as a locomotive at all, but to drive pumping machinery. She had not been a famous engine in her day, and her early sale out of railway service could well have been the last anyone with railway interest might have heard of her. All the same she went on steadily pumping away at Princes Dock, Liverpool for nearly *seventy years*; and then a railway enthusiast visiting the docks on other business happened to see her. She was brought to the notice of Sir Henry Fowler (then Chief Mechanical Engineer of the L.M.S.R.), reconditioned, and was in steam during the centenary celebrations of the Liverpool and Manchester Railway in 1931. After various other appearances at centenaries and other celebrations, she was used in that delightful comedy *The Titfield Thunderbolt*. She puffed up and down the Camerton and Limpley Stoke branch of the Great Western, for Titfield in the film was actually Monkton Combe, and finally

rolled into Temple Meads station, Bristol, under her own steam!

71 **Newcastle and Carlisle Railway:** The 0-4-0 *Lightning*.

At the time when the Act authorizing the construction of this railway was passed, in 1829, it was the longest continuous length of railway so far to be projected, sixty-two miles, and the first to cross England almost from coast to coast. But the Rainhill trials had not yet been run and the steam locomotive was looked upon as a danger and a nuisance. The Newcastle and Carlisle Railway Company, indeed, decided not to use locomotives at all. There was much delay in building the line, and by the time it was opened in 1835 the management felt that in view of the success of steam railways no objection would be raised. But when two locomotives were put to work, an irate landowner issued an injunction against the company, resulting in the line being closed for six weeks. A fresh Act of Parliament had to be obtained authorizing the use of steam locomotives. Our picture shows one of the early locomotives used for passenger working. It was built by a Gateshead firm, Messrs. Hawks and Thompson, in 1837, and as its name suggests, it was intended for express service. It was very much in the Stephenson tradition of the day, but an unusual feature of all Newcastle and Carlisle engines was the rendering of the names in enormous letters extending for the whole length of the tenders.

72 **Marietta and Cincinnati Railroad:** The 4-4-0 *Washington*.

The natural development of the 4-2-0 type, once so popular on the early railways, of the U.S.A., was into the 4–4–0; for this retained the flexibility and good tracking qualities of the 4–2–0 while providing the extra adhesion and power that was becoming so urgently necessary. In fact the 4–4–0 type was adopted so early in the U.S.A., and for a time became so universally applied, that it was known as the 'American' type, just as later wheel arrangements became designated 'Atlantic', 'Pacific', and so on. The *Washington*, built at the Globe works of John Souther, in Boston, had the traditional short wheelbase bogie, inside cylinders and outside bar frames. The whistle was mounted on top of the steam dome and there were two safety-valves. The enormous balloon-type smoke-stack was designed as a spark-arrester. For the colours in which many American locomotives were finished we have as evidence many supremely beautiful coloured lithographs, which were printed from drawings made by the men who actually designed the locomotives. These coloured lithographs were used by the manufacturers to advertise their products, and there is no doubt that there was much rivalry as to who could produce the most ornate and artistically finished locomotive.

73 Paterson and Ramapo Railroad, New Jersey: The 4–4–0 *Ramapo*.

This is another very striking example of an early American 4–4–0, in this case built by the firm of Rogers, Ketchum & Grosvenor, in the 1840s. The design is of what might be termed an intermediate vintage, between the primitive 4–2–0s, with the tall hay-stack type of firebox, and later designs, first with the straightback boiler, and then with a partially-tapered barrel. Again one notes the whistle mounted against the dome, and in this case, although there are two safety-valves, one is on top of the dome, and the other in a position forward on the boiler barrel. The spacing of the wheels is much the same as on the *Washington* although the bogie wheels are much larger, and not only give a more pleasing effect, but would provide better riding. The *Ramapo* is 'intermediate' in another sense, in that the builders had not then reached the stage of adding cabs. When American manufacturers did start building cabs on to their locomotives, there were no half measures about them. They went straight from 'nothing' as on the *Ramapo* to the fully closed-in type used on the *Washington*.

74, 75 Newcastle and Carlisle Railway: Passenger Rolling Stock.

This railway, although somewhat reactionary at first in its attitude towards motive power, certainly had some of the best passenger carriages of the 1830s. The first-class, (Plate 74), may not have been so ornate as some of the stage coach types used elsewhere, but they were well-designed, having stuffed seats, padded backs and polished mahogany arm-rests. They seated only three aside. There were also small features that were much appreciated by travellers: for instance the window sashes were designed so as to be free from chattering when the train was at speed. The spacing of the wheels was, however, not such as to induce the steadiest of riding, and the reason for this spacing can be seen in the second-class carriage, (Plate 75). The wheels themselves were rather large, and to accommodate them space had to be left under the seats. The spacing of the wheels was thus dictated by the spacing of the seats! It is interesting to see that the actual size of the seats, and the knee-space between them, was the same in both first- and second-class carriages. The second-class had plain wooden seats. There was, as usual, the strong difference in colour between the carriages for the different classes. Our pictures show the original colours for first- and second-class, but within five years some additional 'seconds' were built and finished in a claret colour similar to that of the locomotives (Plate 71). Some of the original 'seconds' were painted white, lined out in green. Presumably these were intended for horse, and not steam locomotive haulage!

76 An Italian Second-Class Carriage: 1840

Developments in railway carriage design came gradually in most European countries, though from the evidence that is available it would seem that the majority inaugurated their railways at a sufficiently later date after Great Britain to avoid the most spartan of travelling conditions, for the lower orders. It is true that some amusing cartoons exist of early days in France, where passengers in open trucks are passing their steaks forward to the driver to be grilled on the footplate! The first railway in Italy was not opened until 1839, and while at that time there were many hundreds of 'open' thirds in service in England, public opinion was strongly hardening against such conditions. The smart little Italian 'second' shown in our picture, completely closed-in, and with curtained windows, could easily be mistaken for a British 'first', but for the box-seat provided for the 'travelling porter'. It must nevertheless be admitted that having started reasonably well, continental countries remained static for very many years,

and some grisly 'dog-boxes' were to be found on international express trains right down to the end of the century.

77 Bodmin and Wadebridge Railway, Cornwall: A Composite Carriage, 1838.

This picturesque little railway, which, with its two branches, amounted to only fourteen miles of single track, opened for traffic in 1838. Its principal business was the conveyance of sea sand inland, for use as manure. In 1840 it possessed only two passenger coaches, and some forty assorted goods vehicles. Of the passenger coaches one was the smart little composite shown in our picture; though the colours shown are those used when this carriage was withdrawn for preservation and displayed on a plinth at Waterloo Station, London. Photographs taken in Cornwall when the vehicle was actually in service show it in a most decrepit condition, as though it had never been painted since it was first built. In contrast to the coaches of the Newcastle and Carlisle Railway, the truly diminutive wheels will be noted. These enabled the axles to be spaced quite independently of the seating in the body of the coach.

78 The London and Birmingham Railway: Building the Boxmoor Embankment.

Seeing the earthworks on which the railways of today are carried, crossing deep valleys on high embankments, or cutting through hills, in order to keep the gradients to a minimum, it is sometimes difficult to realize that these enormous earthworks were built entirely by manual labour, with no more elaborate tools than picks and shovels, and no more sophisticated means of transport than wheel-barrows and horses. Our picture shows the technique used in building an embank-ment. Plankways were erected at intervals up the partly-formed sloping sides, and an arrangement of ropes and pulleys was erected whereby horses on the embank-ment-top could haul a loaded barrow up the plank. The labourer was there to guide it, but eye-witnesses tell how an occa-sional jerk might upset the man's balance and send barrow and man over the side of the plank. Once at the top, the filling material was loaded into large trolleys, which were conveyed to the head of the embankment being formed, and then tipped over the end to advance the bank an inch or so for every wagon load tipped.

79 London and Birmingham Railway: A Handsome Underline Bridge near Rugby.

The construction of railways through the virgin countryside of rural England in the 1830s and 1840s naturally caused much concern among those who feared that this new found industrial enterprise would completely spoil the character of the land. From some there was die-hard all-out opposition, but from others requests that where their property was crossed or ad-joined, the structures involved should be made pleasing and to conform with the prevailing local conditions. Our picture shows a small, but picturesquely-designed bridge on the London and Birmingham Railway near Rugby. Robert Stephenson was engineer for the line, but for structures of this kind professional architects were employed, as has already been noticed in such great erections as the Doric Arch at Euston (Plate 37) and the façade of Curzon Street Station, Birmingham (Plate 38).

80 London and Birmingham Railway: Building the Great Kilsby Tunnel.

While Robert Stephenson could safely delegate the architectural adornments of the London and Birmingham Railway to experts in their respective fields, the construction of the line itself required his constant personal attention and super-vision. And of this work there was no more difficult and hazardous task than the driving of Kilsby Tunnel. Our picture gives a vivid impression of some of the work involved, again with the primitive tools and transport then available. The tunnel is two miles long, and to facilitate working, some intermediate vertical working-shafts were sunk, so that the digging could proceed simultaneously from several points. The work, as on other parts of the line, had been let out to con-tract, but the man building Kilsby Tunnel was unaware, as was everyone else from Robert Stephenson downwards, of the existence of an extensive area of quicksand in the hill through which the tunnel was being driven. Once this was struck, water poured into the workings in such volume that at one time it seemed that the tunnel would have to be abandoned. The con-tractor went bankrupt. Robert Stephenson himself took personal charge; his father acted in an advisory capacity, and event-ually by installation of a great assembly of pumps on the surface the ingress of water was controlled, and work could proceed to a successful conclusion. Today the modern electric trains sweep through the tunnel at an uninterrupted 100 m.p.h.; but when riding in the locomotive cab, and coming to those large ventilating shafts through which daylight comes briefly to the depths of the tunnel, I must admit that my mind goes momentarily back to the struggles Robert Stephenson had to get the tunnel built.

81 Great Western Railway: Experimental Express Passenger Locomotive, *Hurricane*, 1838.

In the early days of the Great Western, before the company had a locomotive superintendent, the specifying of requirements for locomotive power rested with the Engineer-in-Chief, the great I. K. Brunel, and in consultation with various builders some strangely unorthodox locomotives were ordered. One of these was the *Hurricane* shown in our picture. It was however not quite such a freak as it first might appear. The main feature of the design was the complete separation of the boiler from the engine proper, so that each could be designed to ideal proportions without the interrelated restrictions inherent in an orthodox type of locomotive. The engine, the boiler and the tender were carried on separate vehicles, with the driver positioned on the engine unit and the fireman on the tender. The single pair of driving wheels were of no less than 10 ft diameter. *Hurricane* was built by R. & W. Hawthorn in 1838. As designed it was not a success, mainly because there was practically no weight on the driving axle; but students of later locomotive practice will appreciate how closely the idea of the separate boiler approximates to the Garratt design. If Brunel had dispensed with the six wheels under the boiler and suspended the latter on a chassis slung between the engine and tender carrying units he would have secured a more satisfactory weight distribution, and overcome some of the troubles from lack of adhesion. There were numerous detail faults and in 1838 the railway world was hardly ready

for large articulated locomotives. Yet in certain ways *Hurricane* and the companion engine *Thunderer*, designed for freight work, represented a glimpse of far-distant developments.

82 Newcastle and Carlisle Railway: 0–6–0 Goods Locomotive, *Newcastle*.

This massive-looking engine was one of a series of 0–6–0s put into service between 1836 and 1846. They were built variously by R. & W. Hawthorn, by Thompson Brothers, and there was only one by Robert Stephenson. All were named, and seeing the very prominent way in which the names were sometimes repeated on the tenders, in addition to the smart cast nameplates on the boiler barrel, it would seem fortunate that *Newcastle* was a goods engine. Otherwise it surely would not have been very long before some passenger mistook the engine's name for the destination of the train, and got taken to a wrong station! There was indeed a passenger engine on the railway named *Carlisle*, but whether it had its name repeated on the tender I do not know. Names apart, these Newcastle and Carlisle 0–6–0s were strong and reliable and the *Newcastle* put in some twenty-two years of hard work on the line.

83 First Steam Locomotive Built in Belgium: *Le Belge*, 1835.

Reference was made in connection with the German locomotive *Der Adler* (Plate 66) to the celebrated Stephenson, *Patent* 2–2–2 passenger engine. This proved so popular that Stephenson's works in Newcastle could not cope with the rush of orders received, and a number of contracts were sub-let. Some of these went to Tayleur & Co., afterwards world famous s the Vulcan Foundry, of Newton-le-Willows, near Warrington, and Stephenson's records show that in 1834 out of an order from the Belgian Government for three *Patent* 2-2-2s, one was sub-let to Tayleur and was actually built as a 2-4-0 Plate 114). These engines hauled the trains at the opening of the Brussels and Malines Railway in 1835. In view of the success of the 'Patent' engines, Stepehenson's made arrangements for certain continental firms of repute to build to the Newcastle drawings; and so the first locomotive to be constructed in Belgium, *Le Belge*, shown in our picture, was built by Cockerill, in 1835. It will be recognised as every inch a Stephenson design, and very handsomely turned out by the Belgian makers.

84 **North Midland Railway:** Belper, An Early English Station.

The North Midland, the most important constituent of the Midland Railway itself, ran from Derby to Leeds. It was probably George Stephenson's finest work, achieved after all the pioneer, and often frustrating experience with the early railways. It ran through a district that was to become an artery of great industry, a catalyst of ribbon development, of factories, mines and quarries beside its tracks. This did not mean that all was subjugated to purely utilitarian ends, and George Stephenson, like his son Robert, on the London and Birmingham Railway, employed an architect of renown to design stations, and some of the major lineside features. Francis Thompson certainly produced some extremely neat and gracious little country stations, of which Belper, built in the local Derbyshire stone, is a pleasing example of one of the larger types. His design for what was originally termed the Trijunct station

at Derby itself, is a masterpiece to which all too little attention is given today. It was heavily bombed in the Second World War but while the tracks and platforms were badly smashed up, the façade was unscathed, and apart from additional awnings remains exactly as originally constructed.

85 **Syracuse and Utica Railroad:** Syracuse, An Early American Station.

Early American railroad stations displayed a great variety of style. Some were no more than huts out in the country with no platforms; others were equally remote, yet furnished with high platforms in what became the standard British style. In the larger towns, the 'train sheds', as they were known, were enclosed in ornamental exteriors, and the example shown in the present picture, at Syracuse, New York State, has a classical portico, and an ornamental tower crowning the entire building. It is interesting to see that this station, designed by Daniel Elliott and built in 1838, has no facility for expansion. There are just two running lines passing through the building, and the interior seemed to have no natural lighting in the form of roof vents or lights. The smoking of locomotives inside so confined an area cannot have improved the atmosphere, or relieved the general impression of gloom.

86 **Leipzig, Germany:** The First Thuringian Station.

This design by Eduard Potsch, dating from 1840, is a rather more elegant version of the totally built-in train shed. The exterior is finely proportioned and flanked by buildings in a semi-classical style, but a most interesting feature from the railway operating point of view is the layout adopted for the clearance of locomotives from arriving trains. The station was a terminus, with four parallel running lines within the building, and extensions were brought out on to the forecourt, and converged to a turn-table. A locomotive on arrival could be detached from its train, run clear, switch to whichever of the trainshed tracks is unoccupied, and depart for the locomotive shed. Like Syracuse, however, this layout gave no facilities for expansion, and early in the present century it was completely rebuilt with no fewer than thirty-six tracks to serve 400 trains a day.

87 Kassel, Germany: The 'Train Shed'.

This example of a continental station, also built in the 1840s, gives a totally contrasting conception of the accommodation considered necessary. The 'train shed' is light and airy, and the whole area was completely open to the public. The contemporary drawing, from which our picture was prepared, shows passengers approaching and leaving in the open area on the left-hand side, while passengers seemed equally able to wander at will from the platform on to the right to the grove of lime trees beyond. Furthermore, although the shallow 'platforms' are shown along the outsides only trains were despatched from the centre road, and passengers entrained from either side as they wished. Structurally, the all-timber construction of the roof is most interesting, and represents quite a masterpiece of joinery. Among early stations, indeed, Kassel must have been one of the most distinctive to be found anywhere in the period covered by this book.

88 Great Western Railway: The *Ajax* Locomotive, 1838.

A description has been given earlier in this book (Plate 81) to some of the queer loco-

motives introduced on the broad-gauge lines at the time when Brunel was taking responsibility for locomotive matters. This extraordinary machine, also, like *Hurricane* with 10 ft. diameter driving wheels, was built by Mather, Dixon & Co. and it would seem that they recommended the novel arrangement of the design and Brunel accepted it. Apart from their immense size, the curious feature about these wheels was that they were entirely plated and without spokes. One can readily appreciate that there would have been constructional difficulties in making a spoked wheel of such a size—although R. & W. Hawthorn seem to have managed it with the *Hurricane*. But the driving wheels of the *Ajax* were extremely heavy in consequence of the plated construction, and what was worse offered a very large area to be effected by a strong cross-wind. What was still worse, both the leading and trailing wheels were also plated. For such enormous driving wheels the main bearings in the frames look microscopically small, and it is on record that neither *Ajax* nor the sister engine *Mars*, did any useful work on the line. They were delivered from their builders in 1838.

89 Northern Railway of France: A Stephenson Long-Boilered Locomotive.

In 1841 Robert Stephenson patented a new type of locomotive which became known as the long-boilered type. It was a successful attempt to secure more economical use of fuel, a softer blast, and thus minimise the emission of sparks. It involved also a complete redesign of the chassis with inside bearings throughout, to produce a cheaper locomotive than the original 'Patent' of 1833. The design was immediately adopted for home and overseas railways, and large numbers were built, both by Stephensons themselves in the Newcastle works, or under licence elsewhere. But while the locomotives were economical in performance, the relatively short wheelbase under the long chassis gave rise to an unpleasant swaying action when the engine began to develop express speed, and a number of fatal accidents occurred through derailments, particularly with passenger engines of the 2–2–2 type. This short wheelbase is very apparent in our picture of one of these engines running on the Northern Railway of France. Nevertheless they became very popular in France for a time, and when Stephensons secured an order to supply locomotives for the Avignon–Marseilles Railway an arrangement was entered into with the firm of L. Benet, in the little shipbuilding port of La Ciotat (between Marseilles and Toulon), so that many of the long-boilered engines required could be built near at hand to the railway itself.

90 Eastern Counties Railway: A 0–4–2 Saddle Tank Engine.

This line, which became part of the Great Eastern Railway, had a difficult start, with frequent financial embarrassments; and as business commenced, various expedients were adopted to avoid all possible capital expenditure. The original engineer, John Braithwaite, had provided four little tank engines of the 0–4–0 type for moving earth and ballast during the construction period, and one of them was afterwards extensively reconstructed by Kitsons, of Leeds, as a passenger tank engine specially for working the Woolwich branch. The loading gauge was somewhat restricted, and so the chimney had to be kept low. But there was much more to it than that. To provide for additional coal, the frame was extended at the rear end, and a pair of trailing wheels added to carry the extra weight. A saddle tank was added astride the boiler top, and a smart, though curious little engine produced. The coupled wheels of the original machines were large for a contractor's engine, but were ideal for a suburban passenger unit. These were 5 ft. in diameter. But having all the various modifications in mind, and the fact that the engine had to be sent to Leeds and back, one wonders if it would not have been cheaper in the long run to build a new engine! Nevertheless, such was the way things were in the early days of the Eastern Counties Railway.

91 Western Railway of France: A Buddicom 2–2–2 Tank Engine.

In Plate 69, one of the Forrester engines of the Dublin and Kingstown Railway was described, and attention drawn to their bad swaying action at speed. At the time these engines were giving trouble, a young Scots mechanic named Alexander Allan was in Forrester's service, and he carried out a very successful rebuilding of some engines of the 'boxer' type that were running on the Grand Junction Railway. W. B. Buddicom was then locomotive superintendent, and he was so impressed with Allan's work that when he relinquished his English appointment to take up a more attractive one in France he began building engines on very similar lines to those adopted by Allan. The full flowering of Alexander Allan's work was seen later, on the London and North Western Railway (Plate 163), but the Buddicom version flourished equally in France. Mechanically, the chief feature of the design was the building of the cylinders into a massive surrounding framework, very clearly seen in our picture. The frames were double at this point, and the cylinders between. Buddicom attached the cylinders only to the outside frames, whereas Allan made things doubly strong by attaching them to both. The French engines were beautifully designed, and built with superb workmanship; they had a long record of excellent service. An example of the 2–2–2 tender type has been preserved, and was brought to London for the 'Festival of Britain' Exhibition in 1951.

92 **Great Western Railway:** An Early Brunel Timber Trestle Bridge.

However queer some of the locomotives he ordered, however faulty his design of permanent way may have been, as a purely civil engineer I. K. Brunel can have had few equals, and Plates 92 to 95 show some of the most interesting of his early works. The timber trestle bridge, which carried a road across the railway in Sonning Cutting, near Reading, shows an economical, skilful and elegant use of basic materials. But the particular interest in this bridge is that it forms an almost exact prototype for the design of viaducts Brunel used in the West of England for carrying the single-tracked South Devon and Cornwall railways across deep valleys and tidal estuaries. For the taller viaducts the piers were usually made of stone; but the fanning out of the timber struts from the top of the towers was arranged in the same way as in the all-timber bridge in Sonning Cutting. The original viaducts were constructed in Baltic pine, and this had a remarkably long life. While the main-line viaducts had mostly been replaced about the turn of the century, when the main line was changed to double-track, many

viaducts on the branch lines survived until the 1930s. Some notable examples remained until this time on the branch from Truro to Falmouth.

93 **Great Western Railway:** The Skew Bridge at Bath.

For all his thoroughgoing modern ideas, Brunel was a convinced lover of architecture as such, and in building the railways he was always mindful of what is now popularly called environment. He never built anything that was ugly, as will be appreciated from the beautiful little engine houses for the 'Atmospheric' system along the South Devon coast, Plate 53. When he carried the Great Western through the city of Bath, he was careful to avoid any disturbance of the ordered symmetry of the Georgian city by taking the railway in a wide sweep to the south, beneath the heights of Beechan Cliff. In so doing, he had to cross the River Avon twice, immediately on either side of the passenger station. It was a picturesque location, and he adorned rather than disfigured it by the supremely beautiful skew bridge, Plate 93. This was a most interesting conception, for the arches are of masonry, while the supports in the spandrels are of cast iron. It harmonized perfectly with the surroundings. In due course it had to be replaced by a bridge capable of carrying much heavier locomotives, but it rendered many years of good service to the broad-gauge railway.

94 **Great Western Railway:** Box Tunnel.

This was one of the most controversial works of early railway days. When Brunel proposed to drive a tunnel two miles long through the limestone of Box Hill, on a descending gradient of 1 in 100, it was criticized as dangerous and impracticable. But Brunel went ahead, and although there were difficulties in construction, the tunnel was duly completed and remains on one of the fastest express routes of the country today. Trains regularly pass through at speeds of around 90 m.p.h. But one of the most curious facts about Box Tunnel, and one that can hardly be considered as accidental, is that on Brunel's birthday, 9 April, the rising sun shines through the tunnel from end to end. The gradient of 1 in 100 falling east to west permits this, though in steam days it was not often possible to get a clear view through the tunnel. In recent years enthusiasts have gathered at the 'halt' station of Box Mill Lane to see this phenomenon. One cannot help feeling that Brunel engineered the tunnel so that this would be so. He certainly provided the western portal with a stupendously impressive façade, which is in full view of travellers crossing the railway by the London to Bath road. It seems that Brunel was intent upon impressing on passengers in the old style the importance of the new way. For some little time, however, the impression was of the wrong kind, and a local coach proprietor did good business in conveying persons who were scared of going through Box Tunnel from Bath to Chippenham, or vice versa, thoughtfully running his conveyances in connection with the Great Western trains at either end.

95 Great Western Railway: Teignmouth Tunnel.

The 'Atmospheric' system on the South Devon line is illustrated in Plates 51 to 53; but quite apart from the system of traction, Brunel had some interesting problems in carrying the line along the base of the red sandstone cliffs between Dawlish and Teignmouth. The cliffs themselves are stable, but there were parts of the line where Brunel underestimated the effects of the sea. A modern poet has referred to the sea in this area 'idly chafing the rocks'; but even after the construction of massive sea-walls throughout the lengths, I have seen a furious sea in winter-time breaking right over the passing trains. The line was at first single-tracked, and was carried through the succession of headlands in tunnels. At Teignmouth itself the line turns sharply to the right to pass on the landward side of the town and follow the course of the Teign estuary up to Newton Abbot, and in cutting through the last of the sandstone headlands there was, as usual, a short, single-tracked tunnel. When the line was widened to provide two lines of way, in the early 1900s, most of the tunnels were also widened; but the one at Teignmouth, shown in our picture, was opened out, and replaced by a very deep, though short cutting.

96 Berlin and Anhalt Railway: The First Borsig Locomotive, 1841.

It has been stated earlier in this book how the first steam locomotive to run in Germany came from England in 1835. Ten years later, if the states of Bavaria and Baden are excluded there were 152 locomotives at work in Germany, and no fewer than ninety-seven of those had been built in England. Of the rest, twenty-one had been imported from the U.S.A., three from Belgium, and only thirty-one had, up to that time, been constructed in Germany. But in the intervening years, a manufacturer who was to be one of the most important in Europe had started business in Berlin, namely A. Borsig. His first locomotive was built in 1841. In competition with the traditional British designs by Robert Stephenson, the American firm of Norris, of Philadelphia had made some headway, with the 4–2–0 design shown in our picture of the *Lafayette*, Plate 56. Borsig sought to improve the Norris design, and in his first production he added a pair of trailing wheels behind the firebox to help in carrying the weight at the rear end. But this robbed the basic Norris engine of one of its advantages, namely high adhesion on the driving axle, and Borsig's first type, as shown in our picture, did not find much favour in Germany.

97 Shrewsbury and Chester Railway: Stephenson's Long-Boilered 2–4–0 Locomotive, 1846.

The long-boilered type of locomotive patented by Robert Stephenson in 1842 enjoyed a long reign of popularity, due to its economical performance; but great care had to be taken in running it at speed, due to its tendency to 'yaw', or pivot about its vertical centre-line. If it was not very firmly coupled to its tenders this could become a most dangerous movement. The engine illustrated in our picture was built by Longridge for the Shrewsbury and Chester Railway in 1846, and when this railway became part of the standard-gauge lines of the Great Western, it was absorbed into the locomotive stock of the latter company. It was after this that the engine got into serious trouble. Ordinarily it was used on light, slow trains, but one day in 1865 when assistance was needed on a heavy excursion train this engine was put on to double-head the regular engine. She was all right when pulling hard up an incline, but the line between Shrewsbury and Chester is sharply undulating, and with express trains, some good speed is developed downhill to 'charge' the subsequent inclines. Near Rednal the pace became too hot for the old veteran, and with a defect in the permanent way, which was not properly protected, this leading engine was derailed and a bad smash resulted in which thirteen people were killed.

98 Henschel & Sohn's First Locomotive: *Drache*, 1848.

It was in 1848 that another German firm, destined to be very famous, built their first steam locomotive. The works themselves, in the town of Kassel, had been established in 1817. Their first locomotive, the *Drache* (the Dragon), was built for a local Hessian railway, and from our picture one can discern that it embodied a variety of styles. The boiler and firebox was definitely of the Stephenson 'long boiler' type, though the short wheelbase bogie savoured of Norris. The valve gear was also American in its style, but the coupling rod was something quite original, consisting of two round bars connected together. It seems to have been well-designed, and a well-built engine, and Henschel's certainly did not fall into the mistake that Borsig made, in reducing the adhesion at the rear end. Even so, the start of the firm in the locomotive building industry was modest. At first, and for several years, they were building no more than four to eight locomotives a year. It was not until the year 1860 that they turned out their fiftieth locomotive—after twelve years in business—and the average output went up to ten a year during the next five years. It was after 1865 that production really began to soar.

99 Paris and Versailles Railway: A Standard Stephenson 2–4–0.

The application of the 'Patent' conception to the 2–4–0 type by Robert Stephenson did not come until 1837, and then the first engines of the type built in Newcastle were all for export—some for the U.S.A. and some, as shown in our picture, for France. There was a design feature in these engines that was a considerable improvement on previous practice. The leading wheels were made smaller, and this enabled the cylinders to be mounted horizontally, thus greatly simplifying the machinery under the boiler. In comparison with the rather complicated productions of Norris, Borsig and some others of the American manufacturers, the neat, straightforward appearance of the standard Stephenson inside-cylinder design was most marked. There was however a detail feature of these engines that has been commented upon by locomotive historians, namely the extreme length of the outside cranks. The piston stroke was 18 inches, which meant that the inside cranks on the driving axle were 9 inches. Yet the outside cranks were 14 inches, imparting a great increase in throw to the coupling rods. It is sometimes thought, though never definitely established, that this was done to give extra momentum to the coupling rods, and help to carry the rods over dead-centre when the locomotive was travelling slowly.

100 York and North Midland Railway: Third-Class Carriage.

This railway, the first proposals for which were launched in 1835, can be regarded as among the most historic in all England. It was the project that set a York linen draper, George Hudson, on his phaeton career in railway speculation and promoting. In 1835 he had met George Stephenson, and learned of the construction of the North Midland Railway between Derby and Leeds, and Hudson determined that York should not be left out of these expansionist schemes. There had to be a York and North Midland, to link up with the North Midland proper, at Normanton. How the success of this project fairly turned Hudson's head is apart from the theme of this book; but the York and North Midland proved an important link in the chain of communication between London, the Midlands and North Eastern England. Our picture shows one of the original third-class carriages put into service after the railway companies were required to provide covered-in accommodation. This rather forbidding vehicle, with only one door on each side, was designed to carry forty passengers, presumably with a number standing between the wooden-board seats.

101 Grand Junction Railway: Travelling Post Office, 1838.

Mails were carried by railway from the very inception of the Liverpool and Manchester line (*see* Plate 39) but the importance attached to rapid transport of mails by the Post Office authorities was developed as early as the year 1838 when the first 'Travelling Post Office' was introduced in January of that year between Birmingham and Liverpool. The vehicle first used was an improvised affair, but later that same year when it had been decided to make the 'T.P.O.' a permanent institution a special carriage, as shown in our picture, was constructed. This incorporated the apparatus for taking up and delivering mails at speed without stopping. The inventor of this apparatus was John

Ramsey, a Post Office official, and as can be seen from the picture consisted of two parts: a traductor arm, which carried the bag to be delivered, and a net to collect bags from the lineside. The apparatus was such that it was folded snugly against the side of the vehicle in normal running, and extended when the location was neared at which the exchange of bags was to be made. The men in the T.P.O. had to learn the route thoroughly, so as to know when the apparatus could be extended. To do it too early might involve fouling some object at the lineside. Even in this modern age there is no substitute for route knowledge in working 'the apparatus' as it is called on the T.P.O.

102 Great Western Railway: A Third-Class, Broad-Gauge Parliamentary Coach.

The passage of Gladstone's Act of 1844 requiring the railways to provide at least one train every day, serving all stations on the line, having third-class carriages closed in, and charging fares at one penny per mile, led to some curious expedients in complying with the law. There were almost completely closed-in carriages like those of the York and North Midland (Plate 100), while the Great Western temporized by building the semi-covered thirds shown in our present picture. If the Y. & N. M. box was expected to carry forty passengers, one can imagine that this Great Western vehicle, twice as long, and broad-gauge into the bargain might carry upwards of one hundred. In later years the Great Western had some corridor third-class carriages seating eighty people each, but then those relatively modern coaches were 70 ft. long. The broad-gauge 'Parliamentaries' were only 27 ft. Having had legislation imposed upon them in the

realm of third-class carriages, the companies were inclined to 'take it out' on their passengers, by running the 'Parliamentary' trains at night, and as slow a possible! In later years the term 'Parliamentary' or 'Parley' came to be applied to any train that stopped at all stations.

103 Great Western Railway: A Broad-Gauge Composite Carriage.

For the benefit of travellers of the higher orders, the Great Western naturally provided much more comfortable stock, and it was on these that the historic carriage livery of 'chocolate and cream' was introduced. But although the coaches themselves were congenial the broad gauge had its disadvantages in another respect. The ordinary carriages on the standard-gauge lines seated, at a maximum, five a side in a non-corridor compartment; and corridors did not, in any case, come until a period much later than the years covered by this book. But when properly closed-in compartment stock was put on to the broad-gauge trains, the carriages seated *nine* a side. One of the pleasures of railway travel is that of being able to see the countryside as one rolls along, but one can well imagine that there was not much to be seen from the middle seats of a broad gauge nine a sider! Brunel is justly praised for his foresight in providing a railway system that would take many more people within a specific length of train; but one feels some drastic modifications to coaching stock design would have been necessary had the broad-gauge survived, and gone forward into the exacting era of fierce competition with road and air transport.

104 London Bridge Station: Exterior

The first railway in London was that which ran to Greenwich, and what more appropriate place for the city terminus than at the southern end of London Bridge itself. The Greenwich was no more than a local line, and it was not until the London and Brighton Railway was built, that London Bridge became a terminus of any magnitude. Then the Brighton Railway built the handsome edifice shown in our picture. It was distinguished by the campanile tower, and the architectural style was mixed. As the gateway to Regency Brighton it might have been built in a pure Regency motif; but actually there was a mixture of classical porticos, and an Italian flavour into the bargain. It was not long before London Bridge became as cosmopolitan in the traffic it handled as in its architecture. The South Eastern Railway, providing the principal route for continental traffic via Folkestone and Dover, was also admitted to London Bridge, and it became the administrative headquarters of that railway, as well as of the Brighton line; and before long the station of 1844, of which Thomas Turner and Henry Roberts were the joint architects, had to be expanded. The courtyard became a seething mass of horse-drawn vehicles moving in and out, and as for the tracks and approaches, they were probably the busiest anywhere in the world during the 1850s and 1860s.

105 **Boston, Massachusetts:** The Haymarket Station.

This solemn, neo-classical façade could be the exterior of a civic hall, an art gallery, or even a church—anything, in fact, except a railway station! But some of the early stations in the U.S.A. had a weighty dignity of their own. George M. Dexter was the architect, and he seems to have tried to outshine, in this creation of 1844-5, the rather quaint style of the station of the

Boston and Lowell line built some ten years earlier. The latter had a somewhat ponderous centre-piece, though no more than half the size of the Haymarket façade, with a couple of Dutch-looking barns attached on each side. The complete foil to these earlier stations in the city of Boston came in 1847, when Kneeland Street Station was built, and though vaguely in the Georgian style it was little more than a three-storey warehouse.

106 **Boston and Maine Railroad:** Salem Station.

It is always interesting to try and trace the origin of any unusual engineering work or example of architecture, and to unearth the remit that was given to the designer. Salem, on the Boston and Maine Railroad would not be a puzzle in itself: merely an elaborate version of the totally closed-in train shed of which Syracuse (Plate 85) was an earlier, and less ornate example. But the striking train shed of Salem was the work of the same architect, Gridley J. F. Bryant, and the same year, who perpetuated the three-storey 'warehouse' of a station at Boston, Kneeland Street. This is referred to, but not illustrated under Plate 105. At Salem the towers and castellations look very imposing, but the photographs from which our picture was prepared suggest that the interior was very dark, despite the array of windows on the front wall. One would imagine these very quickly got dirty from the smoke of locomotives, and once this had occurred they might well have been opaque. The level-crossing just outside was a free-for-all, for every kind of road traffic and pedestrian.

107 **Paris:** The *Gare de L'Est*.

The Paris terminus of the former Eastern Railway of France is one of the *great* stations of continental Europe. It was built over the five years 1847–52 to the design of François Duquesney and originally had six tracks under the station roof. It is of course the great semicircular window that rivets the attention and this, being some distance away from where locomotives normally stood, kept reasonably clean and provided an effective and elegant lighting to the great concourse inside. The traffic capacity of the station was greatly expanded in after years by the addition of many more platforms; but the façade and the concourse has remained. That concourse has witnessed much of the drama of French history. During the First World War the *Gare de l'Est* was the principal departure point for troop trains to the long battle front extending from Verdun to the Swiss frontier, while to railway enthusiasts the concourse was always a place of great interest in having a fine example of a Crampton locomotive displayed on an elevated plinth. This particular locomotive, *Le Continent*, was illustrated and described in our companion volume, *Railways at the Turn of the Century* 1895–1905, as a full working engine. A variety of Cramptons are illustrated later in this book.

108 A Norris Export to Austria: The *Philadelphia*, 1838.

Under ref. 96, the adaptation by Borsig of the standard Norris 4–2–0 locomotive was described. The present picture shows the standard Norris product, built in 1838 for the Vienna–Raab Railway. It has all the usual features, but derives special interest from the record preserved of its colouring. It was the subject of one of the earliest coloured lithographs, and many copies of it were circulated by Norris to advertise the

type of locomotive he was currently building at his works in Philadelphia. At that time in locomotive history, as will be apparent from many illustrations in this book, wood lagging was used around the boiler barrels. More often than not the slats were unpainted but varnished instead, and well polished. From the lithographs of the *Philadelphia* it seems that on this locomotive the slats were painted in a two-tone green style. How long it stayed like that on reaching Austria one cannot say, though later Austrian locomotives were distinguished by a very elegant, though restrained style of finish.

109 Northern Railway of France: A 2–2–2 Passenger Locomotive.

Earlier in this book references have been made to the influences of Forrester, Alexander Allan and W. B. Buddicom on early locomotive practice of the French railways, and this picture, illustrating one of the Clapeyron-type 2–2–2s on the Northern Railway, is a further example of the Allan–Buddicom style. Allan always set his cylinders on a slight incline, while Forrester, it will be recalled, was the first engineer to use horizontal cylinders outside. This Nord locomotive has the haystack type of firebox as in the Stephenson designs, and although the boiler barrel is fairly long, it could not be described as a long-boilered type of locomotive owing to the wide spacing of the wheels. These engines were the first to be built for the Northern Railway, and were constructed by Koechlin in 1846. The driving wheels were 5 ft. 8 in. diameter, and the cylinders 14 in. diameter by 22 in. stroke. From all accounts they appear to have been excellent engines.

When Borsig's adaptation of the Norris 4–2–0 into a 4–2–2 proved unsatisfactory, he changed to a type described as 'English'; but from a study of Plate 110 it could be called English only from its use of a rigid pair of leading wheels instead of the swivelling American truck, and a pair of trailing wheels in a rear of the firebox. This design proved a great success and from its first introduction, many hundreds of locomotives were supplied to most of the German railways, and many foreign ones as well. The details varied, chiefly in respect of the driving wheel diameter, from a minimum of 5 ft. 6 in. up to a maximum of 6 ft. 6 in. The cab shown in our picture was added on locomotives built from 1863 onwards. The outside cylinders were 15 in. diameter by 22 in. stroke, and the total weight of the engine alone, according to the requirements of individual railways, varied between 25 and 30 tons. It was a fairly massive little job for the early 1850s, when it was first introduced. The bright colour scheme was apparently devised by Borsig and applied to all orders when first delivered, and the combination of green with the highly polished brasswork of dome and safety-valve cover led to them being nick-named the *Spinat mit Ei* locomotives—that is 'spinach with egg'!

111 **Philadelphia and Reading Railroad:** The 4–4–0 *Gowan and Marx*, 1839.

This remarkable locomotive, one of the first 4–4–0s ever built, was named, oddly enough, not from its designer nor its users but after a London banking firm. It was built in 1839 by Eastwick and Harrison, of Philadelphia, and intended for slow-speed coal traffic. It was fitted with the hay-stack type of firebox, favoured by Edward Bury in England, and was originally intended to burn hard coal. In this respect it was not a success. The Bury engines in England were coke-burners, and it was not until the invention of the brick arch in a conventional firebox some years later that coal was successfully used as a locomotive fuel. The *Gowan and Marx* did all its best work as a wood-burner. The main line of the Philadelphia and Reading Railroad is fairly free from severe gradients, and it is on record that this engine hauled a load of 101 four-wheeled trucks, representing a total load of 423 tons, from Reading to Philadelphia in 1840. The form of spark-arresting chimney top, designed to work with wood firing, will be specially noted. The performance of this engine attracted considerable attention in Europe, and Messrs. Eastwick and Harrison, received orders for locomotives from the Moscow and St. Petersburg Railway. The *Gowan and Marks* did twenty years of work with its original owners, and after covering 144,000 miles it was traded in to the Baldwin Locomotive Company in part payment for a new locomotive.

112 **Eastern Counties Railway:** Auto-Train, 1849.

The problem of providing motive power and rolling-stock for lightly-laid branch lines did not seriously trouble the British railways until the twentieth century, because there were usually plenty of discarded main-line locomotives and carriages that could be put on the job. It was not until the early years of the twentieth century that the vogue of the auto-train began—usually a light tank engine and carriage semi-permanently coupled together and equipped so that the combined unit could be driven from either end. A variation on this theme was to have a small engine unit built on to the carriage chassis, and some of these units are illustrated in other volumes in this series. But the principle of the auto-train was notably anticipated by Adams of the Eastern Counties, when he built the smart little outfit shown in our picture specially for the Enfield branch. This was long prior to the days when the Enfield line had such a heavy commuter traffic as to demand an intense service of its own from Liverpool Street, via the Hackney Downs line. In the late 1840s the Cambridge main-line trains ran via Stratford, and thence up the Lea Valley, and this little auto-train unit provided a shuttle service between Angel Road, on the main line, and Enfield. The extremely small proportions of the locomotive may be appreciated from the height of the chimney, and what looks like a fairly large pair of driving wheels were in fact only 5 ft. in diameter. The position of the buffers also tends to emphasize the diminutive proportions. The carriage was designed to seat forty-two passengers. The unit worked well, and on a special trial run covered the 126 miles from Liverpool Street to Norwich, via Cambridge in 3 hr. 35 min., an average of 35 m.p.h. How many intermediate stops were made is not stated in the report. In later years the carriage and the locomotive, originally on the same frame as shown in our picture, were separated, and the engine was converted into a 2-2-2.

113 New York and Erie Railway:
A Six-Foot Gauge 4-4-0.

There might have been a 'Battle of the Gauges' in the U.S.A. had this railway persisted in its original precepts. While the great majority of the American railways in the Eastern States adopted the British standard 4 ft. 8½ in. gauge without question, the Erie was laid out for 6 ft. gauge, and a number of locomotives were built for it. This outside-cylinder 4-4-0 was originally constructed by Swinburne in 1848, but in our picture it is shown in a slightly rebuilt form with a longer wheelbase bogie, instead of the characteristic truck of Norris proportions, and a cab has been added. The structural design of this locomotive seems curiously mixed up, with outside bearings to the coupled wheels, and a continuous splasher over the top which provided a walkway for the enginemen leading out of the front-doors in the cab. An important design feature to be noticed is the equalizing lever between the suspension of the leading and trailing pairs of coupled wheels. This meant that the wheels could adjust themselves more readily to inequalities in the track than if each pair of wheels had had its own independent suspension in the frames.

114 Belgian State Railways:
The 2-4-0 L'Elephant.

When the Belgian Government decided, by Act of Parliament in 1834, that railways would be planned and built on a national basis, George Stephenson was invited to become Advisory Engineer; and his influence so far as locomotive practice was concerned soon became apparent. Earlier references in this book have been made to the 'Brussels and Malines Railway'. This was certainly the first section to be opened, and Malines itself was planned as the nodal point of the whole national system, with four lines radiating variously to Antwerp and the Dutch frontier; to Ghent and Ostend; to Brussels, and to Liege and

Germany. The section between Brussels and Malines was opened in 1835, and three locomotives, all of Stephenson design, drew the inaugural trains. The 2-4-0 locomotive, *L'Elephant*, was one of these. As mentioned under ref. 83, earlier in this book, it was one that Stephenson's had subcontracted to Tayleur & Co., later the Vulcan Foundry Ltd. These trains on the inaugural day were driven by English drivers, and George Stephenson was an honoured member of the official party. Although there were three separate trains run from Malines to Brussels at the start of the ceremony, all the coaches, thirty in all, were made into one long train for the return journey, and *L'Elephant* took the lot without assistance.

115 Early Methods of Signalling: The 'Policeman'.

Methods of regulating traffic had to be devised from the earliest days of railways, and there was an immense diversity in the methods used. Some methods of indicating 'stop', by means of red targets, flags or balls have already been illustrated; but in considering some of the different methods used, one must recall the early days of railway administration. It was one thing for businessmen, bankers, financiers and men of property to project and invest in railways, and equally for men like the Stephensons to get them built; but it was another thing to operate them. Railway managements turned to men who were then almost the only group with experience of large-scale management of a labour force in disciplined service—officers of the Royal Navy and of the Regular Army. These officers naturally organized the working of railways on military lines, and in this respect the establishment of

'policemen', or signalmen, to regulate traffic along the lines was a natural outcome. On the London and North Western flags were used, and the following instructions given:

1. When the line is clear and nothing to impede the progress of the train, the policeman on duty will stand erect with his flag in hand but showing no signals.

2. If required to stop, the red flag will be shown and waved to and fro; the policeman facing the engine.

3. As soon as the engine passes, the policeman will bring his flag to the shoulder.

On the Great Western, only hands were used and the indications were of three kinds as shown in our picture: 'All Right', with the man turned sideways, and arm outstretched horizontally; 'Slacken Speed', man facing, and one arm raised; 'Stop', both arms raised.

116 London and South Western Railway: Early Signals.

The need to provide something more than hand-signals was soon recognized, as was also the need to give a positive assurance of 'all right', as well as an indication to stop if necessary. The upper of the two discs, with the completely open portion to the right, was used as an early form of 'distant' signal, giving warning when displayed (as in our picture) that a stop was necessary at the next signal ahead. There was a lamp, sometimes on a separate post, that showed red for caution. When the line was clear, the disc was revolved round on a vertical axis to appear edge-on, and the light displayed at night was green. The same signal was also used at stations, and in certain circumstances as a direction indicator. The lever at the bottom and the chain enabled the disc to be moved from the left-hand condition to the right-hand. The upper position, in this case meant that the left-hand line was blocked. The lower, meant that both were blocked, and if the disc were completely rotated so that the open portion was on the left-hand side then the right-hand line was blocked. If the disc were rotated on its vertical axis so as to be seen edge-on it meant that both lines were clear. The disc was a large one, 4 ft. in diameter.

117 Great Western Railway: Brunel's Disc and Crossbar Signal

The importance of this once familiar and picturesque signal was that unlike all its contemporaries on other railways it provided completely separate and distinctive indications for 'all right' and 'stop'. There was no case of assuming that all was well in the absence of a stop indication. In this respect, Brunel was decades ahead of his fellow railway engineers. The cross-bar was shown broadside on when it was necessary to stop, with the disc edge-on. For 'all right' the whole outfit was rotated round on a vertical axis, and then the red disc was displayed, as in our lower inset view, and the cross-bar edge on. The downward projections at each end of the cross-bar were sometimes used to distinguish between signals for different lines, where a plain rectangular cross-bar might be used, for another line. Sometimes, at level-crossings, a cross-bar with both upward and downward projections was used as a warning to stop that applied to both lines. When first installed, it is remarkable to recall that there were no lamps at night. These were added later, showing white for 'all right' and red for 'danger'. At junctions green was used as the 'all right' signal. The

cross-bars were painted red on both sides, and discs were white on the back.

118 Newcastle Central Station.

To those who use Newcastle Central Station in the course of business, or for other travel, it is perhaps a little difficult to appreciate that this heavily-impressive exterior remains practically unchanged to-day, from the time of its construction in 1846. The station lies at the junction point of four routes: to Sunderland and the South Durham coast; to Carlisle; and northwards and southwards over the East Coast route between England and Scotland. It was originally approached from the south only by Robert Stephenson's High Level Bridge, and through trains from London to Scotland entered the station at the east end, reversed direction, and restarted along their old tracks for a few hundred yards before taking the line to Berwick-on-Tweed and the Border. Only the Newcastle and Carlisle Railway then came in from the west. But by the turn of the century traffic had grown to such an extent that a second bridge across the Tyne was necessary, not only for the through express passenger trains but for freight. So upstream of the High Level Bridge by less than a mile was built the King Edward Bridge, by which trains from the south could enter the station at the west end and proceed to the north without any reversal of direction. This bridge was opened in 1906. The architects of this splendid station were John Dobson and Thomas Prosser.

119 London Bridge Station: Interior, South-Eastern Section.

Although early railway stations un-doubtedly had finely-built exteriors, a present-day observer, taking a glimpse of travelling conditions a century and a quarter ago, would find the scene on the platforms no less fascinating. Our picture showing the platforms on the South-Eastern side of London Bridge gives an impression of a light and airy station, from which it seems that locomotives were kept outside, and the coaching stock backed in. The South Eastern, like most railways of the period, used compact little 'boxes' for first- and second-class passengers, and the thirds travelled in open trucks painted bright green. Some of these can be seen on the train preparing to depart from the left-hand platform. First-class passengers invariably travelled with much luggage, and the rearmost vehicle of the train on the right is a luggage-van. Other indications of the period are the basket-like trolley being used by one of the porters, and the interesting variety of cabs waiting on the rank on the extreme right of the picture. Travel was then a leisurely business, savouring nothing of the high-pressure rush that prevails at most hours of the day in the present London Bridge Station.

120–123 **Robert Stephenson's Tubular Bridges; Chester and Holyhead Railway.**

It had not been without a great deal of competition from rival projects that the Chester and Holyhead route had been finally chosen for the line of the Irish Mail, from London *en route* to Dublin. Strong representations had been made on behalf of a broad-gauge route through Central Wales to a new packet station at Port Dinllaen, by Brunel, and other interests. When the Chester and Holyhead scheme was approved, the constructional work facing Robert Stephenson was relatively simple except in crossing the Conway

estuary, and at the Menai Strait. It was the latter problem that to some extent dictated the method to be used also for the first. At the Menai Strait the Admiralty required the railway to be carried at a height that would not interfere with shipping—though what shipping actually passed through the strait is somewhat obscure. The main point so far as Stephenson was concerned was that the Admiralty were in a position to dictate conditions, and nothing was to be gained by arguing. Furthermore, no more than the very minimum of interruption to the navigable waterway would be countenanced, and this precluded what could have been a normal method of construction, namely building a masonry arch, or arches, with temporary timber shuttering for support during construction.

Stephenson conceived the idea of carrying the railway in tubes that would be strong enough to support themselves and carry the trains. They would be built on stagings at the water's edge close to the actual line of the bridge, and mounted on pontoons that would float. At the appointed time they would be floating out into the water, and navigated into position between the towers. The tubes were made somewhat longer than the distance between the towers, in which latter a channel was left, from water level extending to the height at which the tubes would eventually be fixed. Once in place the tubes would be raised little by little by jacks, and the masonry built in below. The same design of tubular bridge was adopted for Conway, Plate 123, where only a single span was necessary. Furthermore there were not the same hazards of wind and strong tides as were known to exist at the Menai Strait, and the tube did not have to be so high above the water. So in many ways Conway would provide a 'trial heat', a 'dress rehearsal' so to speak for the greater problem of the Menai Strait, and give much valuable experience.

The task of manoeuvring the tubes from their constructional point on the river bank to their place in the channels in the towers had to be done entirely by manpower, and Plate 122 shows one of the tow-ropes being slowly hauled by capstan. It took twenty-six or twenty-seven men to rotate one capstan, in order to provide *part* of the power needed to float one of those great tubes into position. At Conway there were two tubes to be floated into position; at the Menai Strait, as shown in our Plate 120, there were four over the waterway. With the landward spans these could be built without any need to observe the restrictions imposed by the Admiralty. The bridge over the Menai Strait derives its name *Britannia* from the rock of that name in midstream on which the central tower is based. Just as magnificent ornamentation was applied to many of the early railway stations, so the entrances to the Britannia Tubular Bridge are decorated with huge sculptured lions. Plate 121 shows three of them in course of construction in a shed near to the site of the bridge.

124 Gooch's 'Colossal Locomotive': The *Great Western*.

There have been many references earlier in this book to the use of the broad gauge by I. K. Brunel on the Great Western Railway: a 7 ft. gauge, against the standard 4 ft. 8½ in., which was adopted originally by George Stephenson and used by nearly every other British railway. The existence of these two major gauges, and the serious inconvenience that could arise as the railway network developed, became a matter of public concern, and eventually a Royal Commission was set up to examine the whole question. The Great Western representatives argued strenuously for the 7 ft. gauge, but the weight of accomplished fact was against them, and the recommendation to Parliament was that no new railways should be authorized except on the 4 ft. 8½ in. gauge. Brunel and his associates had frequently stressed the superior performance that could be attained with the broad gauge, and in running trials between rival locomotives this was amply borne out. Then, as if to cast the recommendations of the Gauge Commissioners in their teeth, the management of the G.W.R. instructed their locomotive superintendent, Daniel Gooch, to build a 'colossal locomotive' that should easily surpass anything that had gone before, on any gauge. The beautiful locomotive, *Great Western*, was the outcome of this directive, and very shortly after its construction it made a sensationally fast run from Paddington to Didcot, covering the 53 miles in 47 minutes—an *average* speed of 67 m.p.h. from start to stop in the year 1846.

125 London and North Western Railway: The 4-2-2 *Cornwall*, 1847.

The rivalry between partisans of the broad and narrow gauge took some curious forms, even after the Gauge Commissioners had come down heavily in favour of the narrow. One of the strangest efforts on behalf of the narrow-gauge people was Francis Trevithick's *Cornwall* built at Crewe in 1847. This son of the great Cornishman, although a weak administrator, had some of his father's dash and originality, and he produced the extraordinary locomotive shown in our picture. While he did not go to the extent of emulating Brunel's use of 10 ft. diameter driving wheels, he certainly went to 8 ft. 6 in. To avoid having too high a centre of gravity he put the boiler underneath the driving axle. This produced three major complications: the lower part of the barrel had to be cut away from the second of the leading wheels; the upper part of the boiler had to be grooved to clear the driving axle, and lastly, the trailing wheel axle went clean through the firebox! It was, of course, an utter freak, and did practically no useful work. In 1858 she was rebuilt as an orthodox 2–2–2, and took her place among the ordinary express locomotives of the line, though still distinguished by her huge 8 ft. 6 in. driving wheels. As such she has been preserved, and is now to be seen in the Museum of Transport at Clapham.

126 Stockton and Darlington Railway: The 2–2–2 *Meteor*, 1843.

The early history of the Stockton and Darlington Railway is so indissolubly linked with the work of George Stephenson and Timothy Hackworth that a sight of the simple, relatively 'modern' 2–2–2 that is the subject of this picture may cause some surprise. But by that time there was a new locomotive superintendent at Shildon Works in the person of Thomas Bouch, and rather than continue with the double-ended precepts of Hackworth he turned to more unorthodox designs that were by the early 1840s becoming well proved on British railways. The *Meteor*, built at Shildon in 1843, was derived directly from the very successful 2–2–2 of Sharp, Roberts design, dating from 1835. It was distinguished from Stephenson's *Patentee* by the curve of the outside framing over the coupled wheels, and in superficial detail by the shape of the chimney, and the

ornamental dome-cover sitting, on a square-based pedestal. It was not a large, or powerful engine, and its basic dimensions, with 5 ft. diameter driving wheels, and cylinders only 15 in. diameter by 18 in. stroke, compare strikingly with those of Gooch's 'colossal' *Great Western*, which had 18 in. by 24 in. cylinders and 8 ft. diameter driving wheels.

127 London and North Western Railway, Southern Division: Stephenson's Long-Boilered 4–2–0.

After the formation of the London and North Western Railway in 1846, by amalgamation of the London and Birmingham and the Grand Junction Railways, the two main constituents remained very much apart for a time, with separate autonomous locomotive superintendents. To increase the 'confrontation', which matters occasionally approached (!), the locomotives of the Northern Division were painted a sober green with very few embellishments (see Plates 163 and 183)—not to mention the *Cornwall*—while those of the Southern Division were a brilliant pillar-box red. So far as express locomotives were concerned, the L.N.W.R. types represented the highest and most successful development of the Stephenson long-boilered type. By putting the driving wheel at the rear and having the leading wheels widely spaced, a steady riding engine was obtained without any of the yawing dangers that beset those locomotives that had all the wheels bunched closely together, as on the French Northern 2–2–2 (Plate 89) and the Shrewsbury and Chester 2–4–0 (Plate 97) which came to grief at Rednal. These L.N.W.R. 4–2–0s were large, powerful and fast engines with 7 ft. diameter driving wheels, and $15\frac{1}{2}$ in. by 24 in. cylinders. Altogether there were thirty-seven long-boilered 4–2–0s on the Southern Division, though not all of these had driving wheels as large as the one illustrated.

128–131 Creations of Thomas Russell Crampton.

Crampton was on the Great Western, under Daniel Gooch, in the exciting days of the 'Battle of the Gauges', but long before that he had given much attention to locomotive design on his own account and had conceived the idea that to secure steady running, and at the same time avoid having a high centre of gravity, the driving wheel must be kept at the extreme rear end, with the axle in rear of the firebox. The precept of a low centre of gravity was later shown to be a fallacy, if one required smooth and easy riding, and Crampton had some difficulty in getting his ideas accepted at first. The earliest locomotives built to his patents were, in fact, for one of the Belgian lines, the Liege and Namur, and it is one of these, the *Namur*, that is shown in Plate 128. These two locomotives were built in England by Tulk and Ley of the Lowca Works, Whitehaven. They had 7 ft. diameter driving wheels, and the cylinders were 16 in. diameter by 20 in. stroke. Before shipment to Belgium these two engines ran some trips on English railways, but they did not create a very good impression. While they sat firmly enough upon the rails, they rode harshly, and were not kind to the track.

Nevertheless a number of them were tried and out of a batch built, as a speculation one assumes, by Wilsons of Leeds in 1848, five were sold to the Eastern Counties Railway (Plate 129). They were purchased as express passenger engines, but

their early relegation to the haulage of coal trains tells its own tale! But this unpopularity in England is all the more remarkable in view of the way the type caught on in France. While the Wilson engines were giving the Eastern Counties Railway one headache after another, the French firm of 'Cail et Cie' secured an order for twelve of almost identical design for the Northern Railway. This was the signal for the general adoption of the type on the Paris, Lyons and Mediterranean, on the Northern, and above all on the Eastern. On the last-mentioned line it was the standard express locomotive type during the twenty-seven years from 1852 to 1878, so much so that the phrase *Prendre le Crampton*, was colloquial French for going by train! The preservation and display of the last of the Eastern Railway Cramptons, *Le Continent*, has been mentioned in connection with the *Gare de l'Est* terminal station in Paris (Plate 107).

Our picture, Plate 130, shows one of the Cramptons working on the P.L.M. This was a handsome version of the type, though the rapid increase in train loads on that line made it necessary to introduce coupled engines earlier than elsewhere in France, and in 1869 twelve of the P.L.M. Cramptons were sold to the Eastern Railway. It is recorded that in 1855 one of the P.L.M. Cramptons worked an Imperial special from Marseilles to Paris at an average speed of 62 m.p.h. The train consisted of only two coaches, but it certainly shows that these engines could run. Many hundreds of Crampton locomotives were built for service in Germany, and Plate 131 shows an extremely attractive example running on the Baden State Railways. The machinery has some curious features, for example the cylinders were fixed to the *outside* of outside frames. As a natural outcome of this, all the running gear was also outside, and the locomotive must have looked intriguing and impressive as it travelled along. Crampton-type locomotives were introduced in Germany around 1853, but construction of them continued by the famous Munich firm of Maffei for many years afterwards. The *Bardenia*, which is the subject of our picture, was built in 1863.

132 Manchester and Leeds Railway: Early Second-Class Carriage.

This railway was the most important constituent of the Lancashire and Yorkshire Railway, which was formed in 1847, and it conveyed an ever-increasing traffic between Manchester and the Yorkshire towns grouped east of the Pennines. It originally reached Leeds by making a junction with the North Midland Railway at Normanton, and exercising running over the last twenty odd miles. From an early date, the Manchester and Leeds was providing completely closed-in carriages for its second-class passengers, with seats on the roof for the guards who wore scarlet coats and tall black beaver hats. But the merest glance at our picture is enough to suggest that the accommodation must have been extremely cramped. The compartment probably did not seat more than four aside; but even so twenty-four persons in such a tiny vehicle would be no end of a jam. One of the most peculiar features would appear to have been the means of ventilation, with sliding wooden shutters on the doors. When opened these partly obscured the view through the tiny side windows as shown in the successive stages of adjustment in the doors of the three compartments.

133 London and North Western Railway: Passengers' Luggage Van.

One of the great difficulties and hazards experienced in the early days of railway travelling was what to do about the passenger who arrived at the station with a vast amount of luggage. In the case of first-class passengers, it was usually piled on the roofs, always creating the risk of damage by fire. But as the travel habit grew, and persons of moderate means began to use railways and travel second- or even third-class, the accommodation of luggage became a real problem. There was little space in the Parliamentary third-class carriages, and yet the railways as common carriers were bound to convey what traffic was offered. It is true there were limitations upon what a passenger might take free of charge; but providing he was prepared to pay excess luggage charges there was otherwise no limit. The L.N.W.R. sought to overcome the difficulty of luggage accommodation by introducing the primitive form of luggage van shown in our picture. No more than about half its length was roofed over for the baggage, while the hood formed a shelter for the guard. It was not until later that railway companies began to include luggage compartments in the ordinary carriages. Second- and third-class passengers were expected to 'travel light' in early days.

134, 135 A 'Race Special', 1846.

These two pictures, which are based on contemporary sketches, vividly illustrate the contrast between first- and third-class standards of travel. It is true that by the year 1846 the Gladstone Act had been passed, requiring railways to provide closed-in carriages for third-class passengers; but on a 'race special' one presumes the fares were at lower than standard rate, and therefore the third-class passengers could be conveyed as the railway company pleased. In those days there were plenty of people of gentile birth who did not mind roughing it when it came to travelling by train, like the clergyman who once said he always travelled third-class because there was not a fourth! Whether first, second- and third-class passengers were conveyed in the same train on these racing occasions one cannot say; but from the decorum surrounding the one, and the hurly-burly the other, one feels that there must have been some segregation on the stations at both departure and arrival points. So far as the first-class carriages were concerned, the contemporary sketch from which our picture was prepared shows a single-sided *coupé* of a compartment at the near-end of the carriage, with glass windows throughout the tail-end. Such carriages were not common at this period, though of course any kind of stock may have been pressed into service when the rush of traffic demanded the running of extra trains.

136 The First Locomotive in Denmark: *Odin*, 1847.

The first railways in Denmark were all privately owned, and in 1847 the first section was opened—a stretch of twenty miles from Copenhagen to Roskilde; and Denmark then provided yet another instance of a railway system, the first locomotives of which were of British build. *Odin*, shown in our picture, was a typical example of the once-familiar Sharp 2–2–2. It was an essentially simple and reliable design, and it got the Danish railways off to a good start. In 1947, the year of the centenary of the Danish Railways, a set of commemorative stamps was issued by the Danish post office, and *Odin* was one of the three locomotives chosen to figure in the set. The other two were one of the largest steam trains then in service, and a multiple-unit diesel train working in conjunction with one of the numerous train ferries that maintain the continuity of railway service across the islands of the Danish archipelago. So far as *Odin* herself was concerned, the design included just those differences in detailed features that distinguished the early products of the various British manufacturers, all working on the basic soundness and simplicity of design that was derived from the early experience of Robert Stephenson on the Liverpool and Manchester Railway.

137 Lancashire and Yorkshire Railway: An 0–4–2 Bury Engine, *Victoria*.

The distinction of Edward Bury's locomotive practice in comparison to that of Stephenson has already been mentioned in dealing with the Liverpool and Manchester engine *Liverpool* under reference 68. Bury maintained his peculiar style of construction on bar frames, for many years, and until the London and Birmingham Railway began to use the Stephenson long-boilered 4–2–0s (Plate 127), he had a virtual monopoly of the motive power on that important railway. In the meantime, enlarging his locomotives and improving their design features, he sold many locomotives to other railways. One of the most notable examples still preserved is the old Furness 0–4–0 *Coppernob*. The engine illustrated in our picture could also be dubbed a 'coppernob' in view of the large hay-stack type of firebox uprising among the general motif of dark green. A characteristic of all Bury bar-framed engines was their spidery appearance, owing to the absence of the traditional British deep-plate frame. On the other hand the bar frame became almost always adopted for locomotives of American design, down to the very largest in use in the final days of steam.

138 The First Railway in Russia:
A Stephenson 2-2-2 of 1836.

Railways had an auspicious start in Russia. There was no arguing with reactionary landlords; no setting up of Parliamentary Commissions; no obtaining Acts of authorization. The Czar of Russia said that there would be a railway from St. Petersburg to Moscow and an engineer named Franz Gerstner, said to be a Czech, was simply instructed to build the line. And that was that! He obtained all the material he required from England, and laid out the line to a gauge of 6 ft. That the Russians were not partial to any one manufacturer is evident from the first three locomotives being ordered from three different firms—one each from Stephenson, Hackworth and Tayleur. From our picture, which illustrates the Stephenson example, it will be seen that it was of the standard 'Patentee' 2-2-2 design. The old rivalry between Stephenson and Hackworth flared up in a most amusing manner over the export of the respective engines. Both firms succeeded in getting laudatory press notices into some of the local newspapers, and some extraordinary claims for maximum speed were made. Stephenson's was described as 'a locomotive of a most superior workmanship', which had attained a speed of $65\frac{1}{2}$ m.p.h. Hackworth followed by claiming that his engine had run at 72 m.p.h.! Relating to the year 1836 it is hard to believe that either of these claims were accurate.

139 Eastern Counties Railway:
A Braithwaite 0-4-0.

John Braithwaite must be considered as one of the unluckiest of early British railway engineers. He was associated with Ericcson in the design and running of the *Novelty* at the Rainhill trials in 1829; and had the misfortune of seeing their engine, which was easily the popular favourite, fail through a fault in its machinery. He then went into partnership with another mechanical engineer, and at the same time became connected with various civil engineering projects, including the building of the first sections of the Eastern Counties Railway. This was a concern that was chronically short of funds, and he had to lay out the line on the cheapest possible basis to avoid excessive earth-works. He built some locomotives for the Eastern Counties Railway, of which the 0-4-0 illustrated is a typically modest example, and then, from the mid-1840s, disappeared completely from the scene.

140 The Royal Border Bridge:
Berwick-upon-Tweed.

The ancient town of Berwick is perched high on the northern bank of the Tweed, where that river is broadening out into a tidal estuary. The ground to the south of the river is also high, and in carrying the old Newcastle and Berwick Railway across this deep valley, Robert Stephenson had to resort to a long and high viaduct. Its construction has been compared to the first highway bridge across the Tweed at this point, begun in Stuart days in 1609; this latter has fifteen arches, and took just over twenty-four *years* to complete. Robert Stephenson crossed the river at a maximum height of 126 ft. His viaduct has twenty-eight arches, and has a total length of

720 yards. For the piers that actually stand in the water, piles were driven deep to provide a massive foundation, and in all the river work the bricks were set in cement. This noble bridge took three years and four months to build, and it was opened by Queen Victoria in 1850, thus bequeathing the name 'Royal' into its title. Actually it does not cross the Scottish border. The town of Berwick is in England, and the border itself is some three miles further north. The bridge is a magnificent work, and despite the vastly heavier locomotives and trains which now cross it, it remains today just as it was built.

141 A Notable French Viaduct: Morlaix, on the Le Mans–Brest Line.

The railways serving the north-western coastal districts of France involved some heavy engineering work, particularly where the lines were running roughly parallel to the coast and a succession of deep valleys had to be crossed. One of the earliest of these railways, that from Paris to Rouen and Havre, was built by the English engineer, Joseph Locke, with Thomas Brassey as the contractor. They had a disastrous set-back in Barentin, north of Rouen, when a great viaduct more than 100 ft. high collapsed. The reasons for this accident were many and complicated, but Brassey was one of the most upright of men, and without waiting to argue the reasons or the responsibility, he set about the rebuilding at once. The great viaduct at Morlaix, in Brittany, shown in our picture, was built at a somewhat later date. It spans the valley most dramatically, striding high above the picturesque old fifteenth- and sixteenth-century houses that line the river. The piers of the railway viaduct are extraordinarily massive, and at

their bases are 72 ft. by 27 ft. The maximum height of the viaduct is nearly 200 ft. It will be seen that this great 'arcade' has a lower reinforcing series of arches rising to about one-third of the total height of the viaduct.

142 North Midland Railway: Milford Tunnel.

In building the North Midland Railway from Derby to Leeds George Stephenson engineered the straightest, and most level route that could be secured. Generally speaking the line was not difficult, except perhaps on some stretches of the first length out of Derby, where the valley of the River Derwent was being followed. Where there were obstructions, however, Stephenson went straight through. This was to be a fast express route, with no awkward curves and deviations to circumvent hills, and rocky outcrops. At Milford Tunnel between Derby and Duffield he tunnelled under an obstructing hill, and it would have been no more than a very ordinary tunnel but for the stupendous portal at the north end. Why this awe-inspiring façade was designed it is now difficult to say; though more than 100 years later, with the growth of vegetation and the blackening of the masonry, this entrance is much less prominent. Furthermore, facing north it is almost perpetually in shade even on the brightest of days. But it is still there, just as Stephenson built it, and it is only since the introduction of diesel railcars that ordinary passengers get a glimpse of it.

143 Newcastle and Carlisle Railway: Scotswood Viaduct.

The projected route of the Newcastle and Carlisle Railway involved crossing from the north to the south bank of the River

Tyne just after passing Scotswood. Various proposals for a viaduct had previously been made, including that of a suspension bridge. But the proposal that was finally accepted was that of John Blackmore. To meet local conditions the river had to be crossed on the skew, and the design as actually constructed consisted of no less than eleven spans, each of about 60 ft. It was entirely constructed of timber. There is a considerable difference between high and low water on this reach of the Tyne, and the bridge was required to provide a headway of 17 ft. 4 in. above the accepted high water mark at spring tides. Our picture shows the elegant design used for the piers and the spans. The piers, in line with the course of the river, were athwart the line of railway at an angle of about 45 degrees. The bridge carried a double line of railway, and it was opened for traffic in 1838. Its life however was relatively short by the standards of early railway structures, though not through any defect of its own. In May 1866, when one of the periodic routine tests of the Board of Trade was in progress, it was accidentally set on fire, and completely burnt down. A temporary single-line bridge was quickly substituted, but the final replacement was a massive utilitarian hog-backed girder bridge completed in 1868, which is still in service today.

144 Stockton and Darlington Railway: Skerne Bridge.

After mention of some of the great structures being built in railways in the 1850s, it is interesting to recall the amusing story of Skerne Bridge. To outward appearances there is nothing remarkable about it; but the Stockton and Darlington did not have many large civil engineering works, and

the directors, while having every confidence in George Stephenson as a mechanical engineer, had no evidence to judge his ability where large structures were concerned. They suggested that a well-known Italian architect then resident in Durham, Ignatius Bonomi, should be consulted. Stephenson was not interested, having complete confidence in his own plans. But the directors pressed the point, and eventually it was understood that the bridge would be built according to the recommendations Bonomi had made. It was intended to be an iron bridge. Nevertheless the price of iron proved so high, and the iron-founders so reluctant to tender, that eventually the bridge was built in stone, exactly as George Stephenson had designed it in the first place.

145 The First Iron Railway Bridge: Gaunless Valley, near Bishop Auckland.

Despite his triumph over the suggested amendment of his plans for Skerne Bridge, George Stephenson was not averse to building an iron bridge when it suited his purpose, and on another part of the Stockton and Darlington line he built the first iron bridge in the world to carry a railway. He originally designed it with three spans, each of 12 ft. 6 in.; but after a serious flood in 1824, a year before the railway was opened he found it necessary to add a fourth. Each girder was of wrought iron, and consisted of two segmental arches, one curving upward and the other downward. Their ends united at the point of intersection on a cast-iron boss. As our picture shows there were vertical tie-rods between the two curving members, and the uniting bosses rested on cast-iron columns, braced together. This bridge bore the strong imprint of Stephenson's natural genius, in its skilful blend of cast- and wrought-iron members. Unlike some of the later and larger railway bridges it was built economically to serve the immediate needs of the line, and consequently had to be replaced when larger and heavier rolling-stock than before was brought into service.

146 Great Western Railway: The 'Long Charley' Carriages.

Frequent references have already been made in this book to the difference between the British and American approach to passenger carriage design, and how British railways were to some extent handicapped by the early standardization of short individual turn-tables in the stations which could accommodate no more than one, short four-wheeled carriage. The Great Western Railway attempted to break away from this tradition in 1852, when it put into service a set of six composite carriages no less than 38 ft. long and each carried on eight wheels. At first sight it looks as though there were two bogies; but this was not so. The four axles were equalized in pairs, with large outside compensating beams between each. A pivotal action in these beams gave a limited amount of side play. This six-coach train was used on the broad-gauge expresses between London and Birmingham, then running via Oxford. The carriages were for first- and second-class passengers only. There were three first-class compartments in each carriage seating a total of twenty-four passengers, and four 'seconds', seating forty-eight passengers. The seating would seem to have been more spacious than in some broad-gauge carriages. Though notable as the first eight-wheeled carriages to run regularly in Great Britain, they had a main-line life of only eleven years.

147 Carriage Truck for Conveyance of Private Owner's Vehicles.

In the early days of railways, many passengers required to have their own carriages taken by rail, so that they could transfer to road as soon as their destination was reached. The main lines did not always pass close enough to country estates for these to be convenient for those owning their own road carriages. Some wealthy passengers went even further than this, wishing to ride in their own carriages while being conveyed on the railway. Our picture shows a carriage truck on the narrow-gauge lines, but for the broad-gauge lines of the Great Western, Daniel Gooch designed a carriage truck with very large wheels in which the body was between the wheels. It was reported that these trucks travelled very easily and comfortably, and it was this no doubt that made riding in one's own carriage on one of these trucks so popular. In 1849 the Great Western alone had 224 of them. This fashion, in pioneer railway days, anticipated the present practice of running car-sleeper trains, while in Switzerland, during the time when the Alpine passes are blocked with winter snow, many motorists are conveyed in their own cars through the Gotthard Tunnel.

148 Eastern Counties Railway: A Jointed Eight-Wheeled Carriage, 1847.

While the Americans were developing the bogie-type of carriage, and the bulk of British railways were remaining faithful to the four-wheeler, certain designers were trying to get increased stability of travel by experimenting, without much success, in vehicles of much greater length. One such engineer was W. Bridges Adams, who built the extraordinary eight-wheeled jointed carriage shown in our picture. The body was in two halves, resting on timber frames, which had a hinged joint between them. There were no axle bearings as such. The boxes were mounted in bow-shaped steel springs that allowed a degree of side play. Adams built these vehicles as a speculation at his Bow works and he found purchasers not for main-line express traffic, on which the jogging progress of the traditional British four-wheeler was most apparent, but for local suburban lines, such as the North Woolwich branch of the Eastern Counties and the Greenwich line of the South Eastern. They did not last very long, but constituted nevertheless, an interesting early attempt to break from traditions in the way of British railway carriage design.

149 London and Birmingham Railway: A Bed Carriage.

As an adaptation of the traditional type of early English first-class carriage to the needs of the developing railway age, this so-called 'bed carriage' of the London and Birmingham Railway, introduced at the time of the opening of the railway in 1838, would be hard to equal. Externally it looked like an ordinary old-style 'first' of the Liverpool and Manchester species, with a 'box-seat' for the guard, and an open *coupé* compartment in front. But the compartment at the guard's end of the coach, which by day was an ordinary one, had the backs of the two seats at the guard's end hinged so that they could be swung upwards, thus giving access to the space beneath the guard's seat—a 'boot' in effect. At night a pair of poles were inserted, on which a strong square cushion was placed. Two passengers could then lie down lengthwise with their feet protruding into

the boot. The mail-bags, usually carried in the boot, were conveyed in a locked box on the roof. From this description, however, it will be appreciated that although the vehicle was called a 'bed carriage' it was only one compartment out of the three that was converted to a 'sleeper' at night.

150, 151 Contrast in American Station Development: Lowell (1835) and Harrisburg (1850).

These two illustrations portray vividly the extraordinary change that had come over the American railway scene in the course of a mere fifteen years. Lowell is typical of the modest way in which certain railways began their operations. There was a neat, one-sided pavilion, with no more than a single line of railway. It was sited alongside a broad highway in a yet undeveloped town, but the station itself seems to have been built with little thought of any expansion. Then at Harrisburg, on what became the main line of the Pennsylvania system, there was erected a splendid edifice, originally in the style represented by the totally roofed in stations already noticed in this book, at Syracuse (Plate 85) and Salem (Plate 106). At Harrisburg the same general plan was originally adopted, but with four tracks passing through the roofed-in area. But at a very early stage it is evident that the station was 'bursting at the seams' and our picture shows additional tracks for entraining of passengers and mails on both sides of the original central building. The main building no doubt provided an impressive frontage for an approach by road; but this had to disappear when it became necessary to add the outer tracks. The road approach was then made over level-crossings outside the built-up central area, and road vehicles and their horses were parked in the wide space to the left of the locomotive in our picture.

152 **Munich:** The *Hauptbahnhof.*

The original main station at Munich (*Hauptbahnhof*), was designed in a handsome architectural style that has something of a Florentine touch about it. The façade, designed by Friedrich Burklein, in 1847, provides entry to a splendidly impressive interior. Quite frequently what the Americans term the 'train shed' was quite literally that: a plain utilitarian shelter, or partial shelter for the railway tracks. But Munich *Hauptbahnhof* had a fine semicircular arched roof, spanning five running lines, and the supporting members between the basic arched ribs and the roof itself were sumptuously decorated. The outer end was closed in, save for five separate archways, one for each track. It is indeed curious how American and continental station designers favoured this closing in, when contemporary drawings show steam locomotives puffing away to their hearts content *inside* the closed-in area. Munich, as originally built, was a terminus, and it is still a terminus today. The through station, generally favoured in provincial cities in Great Britain, has not been adopted in the development of many of the larger stations in Germany, where the policy remains of bringing all trains arriving in a city into one huge terminal station, and if they have to proceed further, reversing their direction. This practice can be seen *in excelsis* at Frankfurt, Milan, Rome and at Munich, to mention just a few; and the layout thus initiated at the original Munich *Hauptbahnhof*, as well as at many other centres, has persisted.

153 **Brighton Station:** Exterior, 1840.

From its geographical situation it was perhaps natural that the seaward terminus of the original London and Brighton railway should have been laid out as a dead-end. On high ground, at what was then the back of the town, the architect, David Mocatta, designed what is sometimes termed a 'head-type' station. It corresponded exactly in its broad conception to Munich Hauptbahnhof, in that the handsome frontage is at right-angles to the approach tracks. But oddly enough, by the nature of subsequent developments, the traffic working at Brighton partook more of a continental flavour. Branch, or rather subsidiary lines were constructed, extending westwards and eastwards along the Sussex coast, and some trains for these lines entered Brighton station and reversed direction before proceeding. This was the case with certain through trains from coastal resorts to the north of England, originating at Eastbourne, travelling west to Brighton and calling there before proceeding on the direct route to the north. Though Brighton station has been much enlarged, Mocatta's original façade remains today.

154 **Baltimore and Ohio Railroad:** A Ross Winans 'Mud-Digger' Locomotive.

In the early 1840s coal traffic on the Baltimore and Ohio Railroad necessitated heavier and more powerful locomotives, and Ross Winans having supplied some massive eight-coupled engines with vertical boilers to the Western Railroad (Massachusetts), the B. & O. decided to adopt a similar type, but with orthodox horizontal boilers. Between 1844 and 1846 they took delivery of twelve of these engines, of the very curious design shown in our picture, from Winans. The cylinders drove through a very long connecting-rod to a dummy axle at the rear end, and this connected through gearing to the road wheels. These locomotives became nicknamed the 'mud-diggers'—why, it is not now known! Despite their extraordinary features they seemed to work well enough. But why Winans drove at the rear end, and so had to put his gearing adjacent to the firebox, is hard to imagine.

155 A Baldwin 'Eight-Coupled' Locomotive: 1846.

The difficulties under which American railways were labouring so far as track was concerned in early days, has been referred to frequently in previous illustrations and their descriptions in this book. It will therefore be appreciated that the introduction of eight-coupled locomotives—however desirable from the traction point of view—would be regarded with some concern from the viewpoint of tracking qualities. It was with such problems in mind that Baldwins designed the *Ironton*, shown in our present picture. This has an orthodox locomotive drive, direct on to the third pair of coupled wheels, but the two pairs of leading wheels were placed in a flexible beam truck, which allowed lateral motion and permitted the relatively long wheelbase to accommodate itself to curves. This type was also used on the Baltimore and Ohio Railroad. The coupling rods were designed to have a limited amount of movement laterally, to accord with the movement of the leading truck. This device anticipated by some fifty years the Helmholtz truck which was used with notable success on some of the Golsdorf locomotives on the Austrian railways. On his famous 2–6–4 express locomotives, for

example, the leading pair of wheels and the leading pair of coupled wheels were together carried on the Helmholtz truck, and the coupling rods were jointed vertically between the first and second pair of coupled wheels.

156 Egyptian Government Railways: A 2–2–2 Express Locomotive.

In the U.S.A., the earliest eight-coupled locomotives, particularly those of Ross Winans with vertical boilers, were regarded as something of a fantasy. The next example of locomotive practice was a fantasy in another respect. Beneath its somewhat unusual style of decoration, this 2–2–2 was a perfectly normal Sharp 2–2–2 of the type that has been noticed earlier in this book, and which was supplied to many British and overseas railways. But it so happened that Said Pasha who had just succeeded to the Vice-royalty of Egypt was a self-constituted connoisseur of locomotives. He not only required locomotives that would haul his special train at high speed, but they had to be decorated accordingly, regardless of expense. This was not a case of engines being specially cleaned or decorated for special occasions; *his* engines had to be permanently adorned and kept so. With such instructions Sharp, Stewart & Co. really 'went to town' and produced the amazing engine shown in our picture. The translation of the Arabic name was *Saidia*. The engine was delivered in 1856, and beneath its decorations it was a 2–2–2 with 6 ft. 6 in. driving wheels and cylinders 16 in. diameter, 20 in. stroke.

157 Philadelphia and Reading Railroad: A Winans 0–8–0, 1846.

Ross Winans soon abandoned the 'mud-digger' type of 0–8–0 locomotive, and in

1846 he was supplying a more orthodox design, with horizontal cylinders and direct drive. The *Delaware* of this type, had nevertheless a number of unusual features. It used the Stephenson 'long-boiler' technique for one thing, and retained the haystack firebox favoured by Winans in his 'mud-digger'. The compensating springs will be noted, providing easy running on poor track. But the most remarkable feature, evident in the contemporary photograph from which our picture was prepared, was the completely straightback line of the boiler top—entirely free of the usual appurtenances usually found on American locomotives: not even a bell! Nevertheless this type was notable in leading Ross Winans on to the extraordinary 'Camel' type, which came to be used extensively on the Baltimore and Ohio Railroad. This, however, is leading beyond the period of this book, and will be duly featured in the next volume in this series.

158, 159 Austerity Travel on Secondary Lines.

Two pictures under the above references tend to underline the conditions of travel that prevailed in Great Britain even after the passage of the famous Gladstone Act of 1844. The Vale of Neath Railway was a broad-gauge line under the wing and influence of the Great Western. It was primarily a coal carrier, and with the richest part of the South Wales coalfield worked by small independent railways, it was for many years the most important feeder route of coal traffic to the Great Western. Nevertheless the bulk of its traffic was destined for Swansea on the Vale of Neath, and when the Great Western was compelled by law to close in its third-class carriages, it managed to dispose of some of them to the 'Vale of Neath'. These were of the rather forbidding type shown in our picture, with iron bodies, and savouring generally of an open 'coffin' style of travel. The Great Western had hitherto conveyed third-class passengers on goods trains, and the 'Vale of Neath' made good use of these old 'coffins' by including them in the coal trains, and charging cheap fares for the privilege. By charging less than the statutory penny per mile they were under no legal obligation to provide covered or closed-in accommodation.

The little Bodmin and Wadebridge second-class carriage is a remarkable period piece. No windows, except those in the doors, and very cramped seating with one's knees touching those of the person opposite, must have made those who braved the journey from Bodmin to Wadebridge mighty glad when it was over. This little railway could afford no improvements in its stock. There seems to have been no money even to give the coaches a coat of paint, judging from contemporary photographs.

160 Stockton and Darlington Railway: A Composite Carriage, 1846.

One can derive so much amazement and amusement at the way people travelled on the first railways that it is interesting to see how coach styles were developing twenty years after its opening, on this, the first of all public railways. Usually smart little four-wheelers of the kind shown in our picture were all first class, but this is a composite with a difference. There is a single first-class compartment placed between two seconds. It will be seen that the latter have windows in the doors. It is believed that this kind of carriage was popular with wealthy patrons, who travelled with their family, or friends in the first-class compartments, and had servants within easy call in the 'seconds' on either side. One might wonder why such confinements of long-distance travel should be applied on so essentially a short haul business as the Stockton and Darlington. Actually this pioneer railway was in process of greatly increasing its extent by entering into a working agreement with the newly promoted South Durham and Lancashire Union Railway, which involved them in the working of a long and difficult line across the very watershed of the Pennines, to Tebay and Penrith.

161 An Early American Bogie Passenger Car.

In their sustained attempts to provide suitable rolling-stock for the lightly laid and scantily ballasted track of the mid-nineteenth century, the American railways were early to the fore in developing the bogie type of coach. At once passenger 'cars' as they were called began to grow very much larger than their British or European counterparts, and were soon distinguished by lofty clerestory roofs. Internally they were mainly of the open saloon type. In fact, the compartment type of carriage, almost universal in Europe, was very rarely seen anywhere in North America. So far as the general appearance of trains were concerned, the British and American styles were the exact opposite: British, with a tall-chimneyed locomotive and squat four-wheeled or six-wheeled carriage; the American, with the three or four bogie 'cars' towering in height over the slender-proportioned locomotive.

162 Rogers, Ketchum and Grosvenor: A 4-4-0 Locomotive.

Thomas Rogers, moving spirit in the firm that includes his name, was probably one of the best-known locomotive builders of the day in America, and as early as 1852 he had standardized on the wide-spaced bogie, Stephenson's link motion, and what was called in the U.S.A. the wagon top boiler. The locomotive bearing his own name was built in 1860, and included all these features, together with other developments. Leaving out of account the highly decorative finish and the ornamental brackets supporting the bell and the headlamp, notice must also be drawn to the sand-box on the boiler top, so fashioned as to look like a second dome. The dome itself was further forward and had the whistle mounted on top of it. The Stephenson link motion was designed in the works of Robert Stephenson & Co. at Newcastle, and was widely used on British and overseas locomotives. It was one of the most accurate valve gears that had been invented up to that time, and was never superseded generally in Great Britain. Locomotives with this valve gear were being built at Swindon, Wiltshire into the 1950s. The wagon-top boiler was a name coined to describe a design in which the transition portion, from boiler barrel to firebox was sharply tapered. It became a common design in the U.S.A. from about 1855 onwards.

163 London and North Western Railway: An Allan 2-2-2, The Menai.

Alexander Allan was a locomotive foreman on the Grand Junction Railway in Liverpool when W. B. Buddicom was locomotive superintendent. Considerable trouble was being experienced with older engines breaking their crank axles. Manufacturing techniques had not advanced sufficiently for a locomotive with inside cylinders and cranked driving axles to perform satisfactorily on sharply-curved sections of line, and Allan, mindful of the theoretical advantages of Forresters arrangement of cylinders (see Plate 69), but also being aware of their bad riding, rebuilt one of the old 2-2-2s with outside cylinders, fixing them very securely between the main frame and a section of outside frame. This obviated the use of a cranked driving axle. It was so designed that the thrust from the pistons was transmitted almost directly through the main frame, thus avoiding the swaying or 'boxing' action in Forrester's engines. This rebuild of Allan's was so successful that it became the standard type of locomotive for the entire Northern Division of the London and North Western Railway. The 2-2-2 wheel arrangement, as shown in our picture, was used for passenger locomotives and the 2-4-0 for goods. A total of 158 passenger, and 238 goods engines of Allan design were built at Crewe between 1845 and 1858, and all except eight were named. Those names were handed down from one generation to another of Crewe locomotives, and when the L.N.W.R. became part of the London, Midland and Scottish Railway in 1922, no fewer than 200 of the old 'Allan' names were still in use.

164 Shrewsbury and Chester Railway: A Sharp 2-2-2, 1848.

One could scarcely imagine a greater contrast in design or style of finish between the two British and the two American locomotives shown in Plates 162-65 inclusive. And all were contemporaneous!

The Shrewsbury and Chester 2-2-2 shows all the standard Sharp features, but was unusual in having driving wheels no more than 5 ft. in diameter. It was built in 1848 and came into the stock of the Great Western Railway in 1854. This engine, and eight others of Sharp's manufacture were notable as being the first standard-gauge engines owned by the G.W.R. This engine was retained in active service, north of Wolverhampton until the early 'eighties', and even after withdrawal it was not scrapped. For many years afterwards engine No. 14 was kept in the running-shed at Wolverhampton as an interesting relic. Unfortunately the desire to preserve historic relics among the locomotive stock of the G.W.R. vanished with the coming of the twentieth century; not only the old Sharp No. 14, but two very famous broad-gauge engines that had been kept at Swindon were scrapped.

165 Cincinnati and Chicago Air Line Railroad: The 4-4-0 S. Meredith.

This locomotive really takes some believing, not in its design, but in the truly fantastic nature of its finish. Lest it should be imagined that our artists have let their imagination run away with them I can assure readers that the basis of this picture is a coloured lithograph by Brett of Philadelphia, which was published in full colour some years ago in the *Smithsonian Journal of History*. It can be taken as quite authentic. Except that the locomotive has the short-wheelbase bogie of old, it includes 'modern' features such as the wagon-top boiler. The dome, in this case mounted on the firebox, with whistle and safety-valve surmounting even its great height, is a monument in itself; while the Gothic-shaped cab windows and decoration under eaves of the cab roof provide another scarcely incredible touch. Only the great 'balloon' stack of a chimney, and the smokebox were left unadorned. One is intrigued also by the name of the owning railway, which includes 'air line' in its title. One thing is certain: it had nothing to do with aviation!

166–169 **Austrian State Railways:** Locomotives at the Semmering Trials, 1851.

The construction of a main-line railway from Vienna across the easternmost chain of the Alps to provide a line to Trieste, and later to Belgrade and the Balkans was a tremendous task of civil engineering. Karl Ghega was the engineer, and he had to resort to very heavy gradients as well as much severe curvature to get through this extremely tumbled and precipitous mountain barrier. There are approximately eighteen miles of ascent from Gloggnitz to the summit of the Semmering Pass graded almost continuously at 1 in 40. This severe incline was not decided upon until Ghega had visited the United States, and seen steam operation on gradients equally severe, and over tracks less substantially engineered than the Semmering line. But he also visited England, and for a time was inclined to favour the Atmospheric system. Fortunately for the Austrian State Railways he eventually decided upon steam, though there was considerable doubt among continental European engineers as to what would be the most suitable design. Finally a German technical journal suggested that a competitive trial be held, on the lines of the celebrated Rainhill trials on the Liverpool and Manchester Railway; and that invitations be issued to submit locomotives that would perform to certain prearranged

specifications. The Austrian Government agreed to this, and the trials were held in the summer of 1851.

The specified performance was for a locomotive to haul a load of 140 tons up the 1 in 40 gradient at a speed of not less than 8 m.p.h. It was a very tough assignment for the period, and four widely-differing designs were submitted. How different they were can be appreciated from the line diagrams:

166 shows the double-ended *Seraing*, built by the Belgian firm of Cockerill.

167 shows another four-cylinder tank engine but with only a single long boiler. This was the *Wiener Neustadt*—(Vienna New Town)—built by Gunther, in Wiener Neustadt.

168 shows an 0-8-0 tender engine, built by the celebrated firm of Maffei, in Munich. The curious feature of this engine, named *Bavaria*, was the spacing of the wheels to permit of a very deep firebox, with its grate almost touching the ground.

169 shows the *Vindobona*, which was built in the workshops of the Vienna-Gloggnitz railway, at Vienna, to designs by Haswell, who was responsible for many early Austrian locomotives.

Unlike the Rainhill trials in England, in 1829, when only one locomotive 'finished' the course, as it were, the judges were put in a very difficult position, for on the Semmering Incline all four locomotives more than fulfilled the conditions. The Government had offered prizes of 20,000, 10,000, 9000 and 8000 golden ducats for the four best locomotives and after much deliberation the first prize was awarded to the *Bavaria*. The other three all received substantial awards. But the outcome of the trials, again quite unlike Rainhill, was that no one of the four designs was considered suitable for adoption as a future standard. Two years had yet to elapse before the line would be opened, and with the possibilities of steam having been successfully demonstrated, an entirely new design was worked out.

170 **South Eastern Railway:** Shakespeare's Cliff Tunnel.

The final stretch of the South Eastern Railway, beneath the chalk cliffs of the Folkestone Warren to Dover, was considered a most laring piece of railway engineering on the part of Sir William Cubitt, the engineer. For the most part the chalk was stable enough, but the constant wave action of the sea caused erosion at the base of the cliffs on some sections, and this led to extensive landslips. When building the line, in 1843, there was an outjutting bluff, between the headlands of Abbot's Cliff, and Shakespeare's Cliff, which Cubitt decided to remove altogether; and with the assistance of an officer of the Royal Engineers it was blasted out of the way. In Shakespeare's Cliff the chalk did not seem quite so sound as in Abbot's Cliff; so Cubitt took the precaution of driving two single-line tunnels and constructing the arches in Gothic shape so as to lessen the pressure on the crown of the arch. The distinctive shape of these bores, now nearly 130 years old and as sound as when they were first made, can be seen clearly from Dover Harbour, against the chalk background of Shakespeare's Cliff. Our picture shows how the railway was originally carried down the slight gradient into Dover on a timber trestle viaduct supported on piles driven deep down into the solid chalk. This viaduct has now been replaced.

171 **North Eastern Railway:** Selby Bridge.

The original route from London to the North Eastern counties of England was from Euston, following the London and and Birmingham Railway to Rugby, thence via the Midland Counties line to Derby, and onwards by the North Midland Railway. The last stage into York was over the York and North Midland, from Normanton. When the Great Northern Railway was opened to Doncaster in 1850 there was the possibility of a shorter route from the south. At first Great Northern trains to York ran via Knottingley, and thence over the York and North Midland; but in 1871 a new direct line was opened from Chaloners Whin Junction, four miles south of York, to Shaftholme, four miles north of Doncaster. For the most part it ran through level, agricultural country, but at Selby the River Aire had to be crossed. At this point however the new line intersected the earlier Hull and Selby Railway. An interesting existing bridge could be used. There was considerable navigation on the River Aire, with tall-masted sailing-ships, and the bridge had had to be designed to give a clearway to ships when necessary. Our picture shows the original lifting bascule bridge, opened for railway traffic in 1840. The balance weights can be seen extending below railway level, with the bridge in the open position. This structure was later replaced by a swing bridge, and this latter is still in service today.

172 **Leeds Northern Railway:** Bramhope Tunnel.

The Leeds Northern was an important constituent of the North Eastern Railway, formed in 1854. It struck out north from Leeds through very hilly country to make a course for Harrogate, Ripon, Northallerton and Teeside. To pierce the high ridge that lies between the valleys of the Aire and the Wharfe there is first of all a heavy climb out of Leeds, and then comes the lengthy Bramhope Tunnel, two miles long, on a gradient descending throughout at 1 in 94. The northern portal of this tunnel, which was opened for traffic in 1849, lies in a deeply wooded glen near the village of Arthington, and a magnificent castellated entrance was built. At the time of opening of the railway the cutting, recovering from all the heavy excavation work involved in the construction, looked fairly bare, and something like the aspect shown in our picture. But in the 120 years that have since elapsed the vegetation has grown and encroached to such a degree that the castellations are partly obscured. The fine stonework has also become much blackened from the effects of 100 years of steam. Trains entering the tunnel, travelling towards Leeds, were pounding hard up the gradient, and the blackening is much more pronounced over the left-hand than over the right-hand track.

173 Eastern Railway of France: Viaduct at Chaumont.

Some magnificent and spectacular engineering works are to be seen on the French railways, particularly where deep valleys have to be crossed in hilly country. As a matter of history, many of these structures offered highly vulnerable targets for enemy air attack during the concluding stages of the Second World War, when sustained attempts were made to disrupt communications. The speed with which damaged viaducts were repaired was one of the engineering phenomena of the period. Reverting to much earlier days however, the viaduct in the valley of the Marne, near Chaumont, while a splendid structure in itself, provides an interesting comparison to the viaducts at Berwick-upon-Tweed and at Morlaix (Plates 140 and 141) which were designed by English engineers. At Berwick the arches are open and continuous to the lowest level, whereas at Chaumont it will be seen that two levels of small intermediate arches are interposed; and to afford a continuous way-through at that level small gateways are provided in the main piers. This method of construction provides an access way, at two different levels, for inspection and maintenance of the fabric of the main structure, and would facilitate the erection of scaffolding when pointing, or other repair work, is necessary.

174 Early Semaphore Signals.

When the principle of the old Admiralty semaphores (Plate 58) was adapted to railway use signals corresponding to the hand signals of the policemen (Plate 115) were given, to indicate 'stop', 'caution' and 'all right'. Unlike the policeman's attitude however the early idea of no signal at all for 'all right' at first prevailed, and with the primitive flags and targets of Plates 59, 60 and 61. The present picture shows early semaphore indications in railway signalling in Great Britain: horizontal for 'stop'; inclined, for 'caution', and hanging vertically down and obscured, for 'all right'. It will however be immediately seen that if the chain broke, the arm would fall to the 'all right' position, and set up dangerous conditions. The arm working in a slot in the post was an essential feature of this form of signal, however, and it is interesting to recall for how long the slotted posts remained a standard feature on some British Railways, long after the obscured 'all right' indication had been abandoned. The North Eastern Railway retained slotted posts as standard practice until the mid-1920s, installing new ones until 1926 at least; with these the usual British indication, with two positions only, of horizontal for 'stop' and inclined downwards for 'proceed', were used. The slotted posts had the disadvantage that they could more easily become clogged up with frozen snow.

175 The American 'Highball' Signal.

This must not be confused with the occasional British use, in early days, of a red ball hoisted up to signify danger (Plate 61). The American signal had exactly the opposite meaning. It originated on the old New Castle and Frenchtown Railroad, that eventually became part of the Pennsylvania system. The first 'ball' signals were installed as early as the mid-1830s, and unlike the British type were of two colours. A white ball hoisted up to the top of the mast indicated line clear, while a black ball run up only half-way indicated 'stop'. The arrangement had a safety feature that the corresponding English type did not possess. If the cord broke, and the white ball fell, a driver would not have any authority to proceed. This use of balls led to one of the commonest terms in American railway operating jargon. The 'highball' became the general term for line clear, and one often saw pictures of trains at speed which were described as an express 'high-balling' through such and such a station. Even today one hears American railwaymen say 'highball', when their British counterparts would say 'right-away'.

176 **Great Western Railway:** The 4-2-2 *Iron Duke*, 1847, 'Lord of the Isles' class.

The great success of Daniel Gooch's 'colossal' locomotive, the *Great Western* (Plate 124), was tempered somewhat when she broke her leading axle; and so, in developing the design for general use on the line, Gooch changed to the 4-2-2 wheel arrangement. The leading wheels were not however carried on a bogie; both axles had bearings in the main frames, and the contrast in this respect between contemporary American design, which sought flexibility in almost every way, and this new Great Western 4-2-2, is a reflection upon the wonderfully straight and well-maintained permanent way that Brunel had bequeathed upon the G.W.R. The first of these very famous engines was built in 1847; this was the *Iron Duke*, the subject of our picture. The *Lord of the Isles*, which was built in 1850, and shown at the Great Exhibition of 1851, was the twenty-first of the class, and by the end of 1855 a total of twenty-nine were in service. They remained the principal express locomotives of the Great Western throughout the broad-gauge era, so much so that from 1878 onwards a further fifteen were built new at Swindon to replace a like number of the older ones that had been withdrawn. At the time of the final conversion of the broad gauge, in 1892, there were twenty-three of them in traffic. The *Lord of the Isles* had been withdrawn in 1884 and preserved at Swindon. She was displayed at the Edinburgh Exhibition in 1890, and at the Chicago Exhibition in 1893. It was indeed a tragedy that the decision was taken to scrap her in 1906. The later engines of the class were fitted with cabs, and older ones that remained in service also had this provision from the 1870s onwards. The polished wooden lagging on the boiler was only used for the earliest engines of the class.

177 David Joy's Masterpiece: The 2–2–2 *Jenny Lind*.

The designing of the first of this famous type of locomotive is one of the romances of British railway history. David Joy was working for E. B. Wilson & Co. of the Railway Foundry, Leeds in 1847. When the Brighton Railway required some new locomotives, he was sent to Brighton to obtain information as to the size and power of the locomotives they needed. But any information Joy had gathered during his visit was virtually thrown to the winds, because Wilson's were afterwards told to supply whatever they liked. At this there was much disagreement among the directors of Wilsons as to what they wanted to supply and Joy, who after all was only an employee, felt thoroughly frustrated. At the weekend following the argument he thought over the problem anew In the quiet of his own home and by Sunday evening the general scheme of the new 2–2–2 express engine was fully worked out. The *Jenny Lind*, for such the engine was named, differed from contemporary types in having inside bearings for the driving wheels, and outside framing and bearings for the leading and trailing wheels. She was an immense success, and Wilsons supplied 'Jennys' to many railways afterwards. At the height of this activity, production of these 2–2–2s from the Railway Foundry reached one per week. In slightly later years 2–2–2 which had this particular arrangement of framing came to be called a 'Jenny Lind', though actually it was only those from Wilsons,

with the classical fluted style of the dome and safety-valve column, that strictly belonged to this most famous series of locomotives.

178 Western Railway of France: *L'Aigle*.

The illustrations in this book have included several of locomotives that cannot be described as other than freaks. Nearly all of these arose out of a desire on the part of the designer to use exceptionally large driving wheels, such as 10 ft. on some of the early Great Western types, and 8 ft. 6 in. on the *Cornwall*. This picture shows an equally extraordinary French example built at the works of Gouin, of Paris, and shown at the Paris Exhibition of 1855. This had coupled wheels of 9 ft. 4 in. diameter, and like the *Cornwall* in its original form, the boiler was beneath the driving axles. This boiler was not quite such a fantastic assembly of potential trouble as that of the *Cornwall*, but it was nevertheless a complicated mass of joints and bits and pieces. Another extraordinary feature of this locomotive was the length of the piston stroke. At a time when most locomotives had cylinders with a stroke between 20 and 24 in., those of *L'Aigle* had no less than $31\frac{1}{2}$ in. One can hardly imagine that the engine did much useful work.

179 Locomotive of the First Swiss Railway, 1847.

The first Swiss railway ran from Zürich to Baden, a distance of $14\frac{1}{2}$ miles, and it soon became nicknamed the 'Spanische-Brotli Bahn', or Spanish Bun Railway, because the so-called Spanish buns produced in Baden were a highly appreciated delicacy in the city of Zürich. They had previously been conveyed by road. The development of railways in Switzerland did not progress very rapidly at first, because the autonomous character of the various cantons had set up numerous trade barriers and tariffs, and no one else was interested in a railway that had originated in Zürich. It was not until after the establishment of the Swiss Confederation in 1848 that these toll barriers were abolished, and in 1850 the Swiss Government invited Robert Stephenson to advise on the setting up of a comprehensive railway system. The first locomotive in Switzerland, on the Spanish Bun Railway, was actually a Stephenson product, being of the celebrated long-boiler type. It has been preserved, and at the time of the Swiss railway centenary in 1947 worked a replica train.

180 **London and North Western Railway:** A Southern Division McConnell 0-6-0.

When J. E. McConnell was appointed locomotive superintendent of the Southern Division of the L.N.W.R. in 1846 he took over a miscellaneous collection of engines ranging from little bar-framed Bury 2-2-0s and 0-4-0s to the first of the Stephenson long-boilered 4-2-0s. His own engines represented a tremendous advance in power over previous standards. He was essentially a 'big-engine' man, and the 'Wolverton Goods' 0-6-0 shown in our picture was in striking contrast to the standard Allan 2-4-0 goods engines of the Northern Division of the L.N.W.R. The boiler was much larger; the boiler pressure was 150 lb. per sq. in. against 120, and the total weight of engine alone in working order was $26\frac{1}{2}$ tons, against $19\frac{1}{2}$. The tractive power was 75 per cent greater. They were fast-running engines too, and their coupled wheels of 5 ft. 6 in. diameter were

nearly as large as those of many locomotives of the day designed purely for express passenger traffic. McConnell's own express engines were absolute 'flyers', and with them he told the directors of the L.N.W.R. that he was prepared to run the 112 miles from Euston to Birmingham (Curzon Street) in the level two hours if necessary. This was in the early 1850s. As to the Wolverton Goods 0-6-0s, no fewer than 107 were built between 1854 and 1863.

181 **New South Wales Government Railways:** The First Steam Locomotive.

The fame of McConnell and his locomotives spread far and wide. He was a founder member of the Institution of Mechanical Engineers and took a prominent part in the early transactions of that Institution. He resigned from his post on the L.N.W.R. in 1861, and was then much in demand as a consultant. But for some time before then he had been consulting engineer to what was first known as the Sydney Railway Company, which ran between Sydney and Parramatta; and when that company ordered four locomotives from England, and specified that these should be of the 0-4-2 type, McConnell simply took his standard Wolverton Goods, the first of which were then under construction, and substituted a pair of trailing wheels for the rear pair of coupled wheels. As will be seen from a comparison of Plates 180 and 181, the engines were practically identical, except in their colouring. The London and North Western engines were at work first, in 1854, and the Australian 0-4-2s were at work early in 1855. On McConnell's recommendation, one of his own men from Wolverton, W. Scott, went out to Australia to supervise the erection of the engines, and they were an immediate success. The only trouble with them was that they were far more powerful than the Australian railway needed, even though the boiler pressure was kept to 120 lb. per sq. in., as compared with 150 lb. on the Wolverton engines. For some time afterwards, locomotives built for New South Wales were of rather lighter design.

182 **London and North Western Railway:** The 2–2–2 *Watt*, 'Lady of the Lake' Class.

This engine, and that illustrated in Plate 183, were both connected with incidents in the American Civil War, and their contrasting designs are of particular interest. The L.N.W.R. engine *Watt* was one of John Ramsbottom's elegant 7 ft. 6 in. 2–2–2s of the 'Lady of the Lake' class, and finished in the sombre green of the Northern Division that was in such contrast to McConnell's red engines from Wolverton (Plate 180). The fame of *Watt*, rests upon a specially fast run she made from Holyhead to Stafford on 7 January 1862. Great indignation had arisen in England when two representatives of the Southern States, sailing in the British steamer *Trent*, had been seized from under the protection of the British flag by a United States warship. An ultimatum had been sent from London to Washington, which if its demands had not been accepted was tantamount to a declaration of war. Great tension prevailed while the reply was awaited. The dispatch containing it would come by the route of the ordinary American Mail, via Queenstown, Dublin, Kingstown and the Irish Mail route to London, via Holyhead. From New Year's Day 1862 the L.N.W.R. kept an express engine continually in steam ready for instant departure. On the day concerned this engine was *Watt*, and she ran the 130½ miles to Stafford non-stop in 144 minutes, at an average speed of 54¼ m.p.h. She was enabled to run this long distance non-stop because the first water-troughs anywhere in the world had recently been laid down at Aber, on the North Wales coast, and she was able to take up water without stopping. The American reply to the British ultimatum was conciliatory, and in the general rejoicing *Watt* and the water-troughs came in for a good deal of praise.

183 **Western and Atlantic Railroad:** The *General*.

The *General* was a standard Rogers 4–4–0, burning wood, and having cylinders 15 in. by 24 in. driving coupled wheels 5 ft. in diameter. It would have been just another 4–4–0 but for a most exciting affair in April 1862, at the height of the Civil War. A party of Federal troops, with the idea of cutting off communication between Atlanta (Georgia) and Chattanooga, made a dash for Kennesaw, a station about thirty miles north of Atlanta. They seized the locomotive *General*, and drove it for all its worth for eighty-seven miles over a typical light and sinuous American track with little or no ballast. The locomotive had no sooner been seized and driven away than a party of Confederate troops mounted a similar engine the *Texas*, and gave chase. So ensued what is sometimes referred to as 'The Great Locomotive Chase', with the *Texas* at a disadvantage in being tender first. There was no time nor opportunity to turn round. Both locomotives were at times driven at speeds up to 60 m.p.h., but in the heat of such a chase the likelihood of derailment at such speeds did not enter anyone's head. The *General* was eventually caught and recaptured, because the raiders had run completely out of fuel. They were then within twenty miles of Chattanooga. Both locomotives involved in the chase have been preserved.

184 New Haven, Connecticut: Union Station.

In looking at this remarkable station exterior, and learning that it was built as early as 1848–9, it is difficult to know whether to be more impressed by the sheer beauty of the architecture, or by the lavish size, for what was then no more than a modest line of railway. The style of architecture, by Henry Austin, was Italian, but quite apart from the actual building, the provision for passengers sounds more like that of a modern luxury hotel than a railway station of 120 years ago. In a contemporary account we read: 'The grand entrance for passengers is from Union Street by a spacious doorway. On either side of the main hall, or platform, are extensive Parlors, that on the left side being for the accommodation of ladies and is furnished with a profusion of rich and costly sofas, divans, chairs, ottomans, mirrors, etc., with convenient dressing-rooms attached. Obliging servants are always in attendance. The Ticket Office is on the left side of the grand hall, with ornamental windows of ground glass. In the North Tower at an elevation of 90 ft. above the street, is a clock, with glazed faces 8 ft. in diameter looking toward the four cardinal points. This clock is to be illuminated with gas. Twenty feet above the clock a large bell is suspended, the ringing of which indicates the arrival and departure of trains . . .' But then we read: 'A watchman being stationed in the building at night, this bell is usually the first to sound its alarm in cases of fire . . .' as if fires were common occurrences! For all this, however, this remarkable station became outdated, and in 1874 was replaced by a still larger one. Austin's elegant Italian creation then became demoted to the indignity of a market.

BIBLIOGRAPHY

BOOKS

C. Hamilton-Ellis, *Nineteenth Century Railway Carriages*, Modern Transport, London, 1949.

O. S. Nock, *The Railway Engineers*, B. T. Batsford, London, 1955.

John Rowland, *George Stephenson*, Odhams Press, London, 1954.

J. G. H. Warren, *A Century of Locomotive Building*, The Locomotive Publishing Co. Ltd., London, 1923.

P. Weil, *Les Chemins de Fer*, Larousse, Paris, 1964.

John H. White, jun., *American Locomotives*, The Johns Hopkins Press, Baltimore, 1968.

PERIODICALS

The Railway Magazine, I.P.C. Business Press Ltd.

The Railway Engineer, I.P.C. Business Press Ltd.

The Locomotive Magazine, Locomotive Publishing Co. Ltd.

INDEX